PROGRESSION THROUGH REFLECTION

A 90 Day Journal For Self-Reflection & Goal Tracking

BLAKE C. HOLLAWAY

Book Cover by Blake C. Hollaway
Progression Through Reflection: A 90 Day Journal For Self-Reflection & Goal Tracking | Blake C. Hollaway - 1st ed

ISBN: 979-8-9903840-1-9 (paperback)

This journal is dedicated to the best version of you, as defined by you.

A Note From The Author:

Hello Beautiful Soul,

I believe there are no coincidences. If this journal has found its way to you, it has arrived at the right time. Congratulations on the journey you are about to begin over the next 90 days.

I originally wrote this journal as a tool to help myself. I am naturally a curious and ambitious person, which means I am always on the go. But I found I was struggling with feeling disconnected, off balance and often burnt out. Though I had regular journal practices, I still felt as if I was thriving in one or certain areas of my life while neglecting another. For a long time, I thought I was lacking discipline and was stuck in the hamster wheel of hustle culture. I felt guilty for resting or would get struck with crippling anxiety attacks whenever I tried to slow down. Something as simple as sitting on a beach for an hour would have my chest tight, heart racing and thoughts spiraling. Finally, I decided a life so full of stress that it overshadows everything else was not the way I wanted to live. I needed a massive change and thus I unwittingly drafted what would later become the foundation for not only this journal but my other guided journal, *The Break Up Journal A Guide To Get Over Your Ex & Fall Back In Love With Yourself.*

What I found after starting this reflection practice was transformative. I found it was so much easier to self regulate. I found that on days I did not meet my goals, it was more often due to completing something else that aligned with a greater vision I had for myself than it was procrastination, a lack of focus, or a lack of discipline. I realized there were days when I completed tasks, only to become so absorbed in my routines that I forgot I had finished them, slipping into a thought spiral where I chastised myself for a supposed lack of progress. Suddenly, my views on success and progress were changing. I was becoming aware of default settings I hadn't realized I had been operating under. And through redefining success and progress on my own terms, I was able to find fulfillment in the journey rather than just chasing the potential happiness in a future destination where the goal posts always moved the second I arrived.

In all, I can't emphasize enough how important checking in with yourself can be for your personal wellbeing. Learning how to hold space for yourself is not an impossible feat or something designated for only a certain type of person. It is a skill that is cultivated through nurturing. So if you identify with anything I said above, you are not alone. Learning to cultivate this skill made me realize the importance of passing on this wisdom. I am happy to introduce you to Progression Through Reflection.

As you set off on your 90 day journey, I want you to know I am so happy you are here and so proud of the efforts you are putting into creating an abundant life for yourself. As always, may your life be full of light, full of love, abundance, and gratitude.

All My Love & Gratitude,

Blake Hollaway

Table of CONTENTS

Table of CONTENTS CONT'D

How To Use This Journal

This 90-day journal is designed to support intentional living. Inside, you'll find prompts for reflection, goal tracking, and habit-building, all grounded in my Four Pillars of Wellness to help you grow while staying centered. You can begin whenever you're ready, and while the journal includes daily, weekly, and monthly check-ins with reflection exercises every other day, you're free to move at the pace that feels right for you. Daily and weekly exercises generally take roughly fifteen to twenty-five minutes while monthly exercises generally take thirty to forty-five minutes. Each exercise is meant to help you build consistency, notice patterns, and connect more fully with yourself. Skip any questions that don't apply or resonate with you.

Your WHY?

A central focus of this journal is understanding your "**Why**." For every goal, habit, gratitude moment, or intention, ask yourself: **Why**? **Why** is this important? **Why** do I want to build or break this habit? **Why** am I grateful? Your "**Why**" connects you to the root energy behind your desires and keeps you motivated even when challenges may arise. Exploring your "**Why**" makes your actions more intentional and aligned with your true priorities.

Root Energy

Root energy is the underlying force or foundation behind a desire or need. Work to identify this energy. It pays off by providing clarity and helps you approach your goals and self-care with intention and accuracy. When root energy is overlooked, you may find yourself pursuing something that doesn't truly meet your needs or desires—for example, chasing money when what you really seek is security. By recognizing your root energy, you open the door to more meaningful and sustainable ways to fulfill your desires and meet your unique needs.

Gratitude & Affirmations

If you don't already have a daily gratitude practice, this is a perfect place to start. Readers of my previous work, *The Break Up Journal: A Guide to Get Over Your Ex & Fall Back In Love With Yourself,* know how much I rave about the transformative properties of gratitude and affirmations. Practicing gratitude can ease stress, boost mood, and create patterns of positivity in your life. Writing down why you feel grateful strengthens this practice and helps you identify and connect to your root energy.

Affirmations—short, present-tense statements—appear at the end of each daily reflection along with a space for additional notes. They help counter negative thoughts, reinforce positive beliefs, and align your mind and energy with what you want to cultivate. Feel free to speak the affirmations I have provided, write them in the note section, make your own or adapt them to fit your journey— use what resonates and leave what doesn't.

My Four Pillars of Personal Wellness:

It is my belief that personal wellness is built and maintained through a strong, balanced foundation of self. Over the years, my pursuit of balance, self-regulation, desire to live in the present, desire for intentional living, and the desire to show up more fully for others — as well as to create a safe and trustworthy space for myself — led me to begin observing and categorizing my inner experiences. Through this process, I began to recognize different aspects of myself, which eventually formed the framework I now call my Four Pillars of Personal Wellness.

By sharing this framework, I hope you discover ways to nurture your own balance and create a foundation that supports both your wellbeing and the way you show up in the world.

MY 4 PILLARS OF PERSONAL WELLNESS

Emotional	Mental
The Emotion Pillar focuses on your emotional wellbeing, managing mood and your sense of belonging.	The Mental Pillar focuses on your mental wellbeing, positive decision making, and rational thinking.
Physical	Spiritual
The Physical Pillar focuses on financial stability, material support, physical needs physical safety, and physical wellbeing.	The Spiritual Pillar focuses on your spiritual wellbeing and connectedness, grounding, power of creation, and ability to be present in the moment. Your priorities and values.

Some tips before you get started:

—— Tip 1

Don't Attach Your Happiness or Self Worth To The Outcome

When striving for an extraordinary life, it's easy to get caught in the intensity of highs and lows. True fulfillment, however, often comes from consistency, steadiness, and calm.

When we tie happiness and self-worth to success or achievement, rest can start to feel like laziness, and the present moment slips by as we constantly live for the future. This creates a cycle of seeking external validation without ever feeling truly satisfied.

Breaking free means grounding your happiness, self-esteem, self-image, and sense of worth in the present—independent of accomplishments or outcomes.

It's easy to forget that you are not alone. Lean on your community and support system—reach out when you need help, and delegate tasks when time feels limited. It's also okay to seek professional guidance; teachers, coaches, and licensed medical professionals can offer valuable tools and support on your journey. You do not need to suffer in silence.

—— Tip 2

It's Okay To Ask For & Seek Help

—— Tip 3

Be Honest With Yourself. Dishonesty Is A Disservice To Yourself & Others

To cultivate authentic energy, it is essential to approach your desires, needs and emotions with honesty. Give yourself permission to feel fully and express yourself openly. Create a safe and nurturing space within this journal—one where your authentic needs and desires can be genuinely seen, heard, and acknowledged. Above all, hold space for yourself and remember you deserve to nurture your own wellbeing.

When we undergo change and progress, we often envision how it will unfold and what the outcome will look like. We imagine a clear separation between our present situation and the new reality, anticipating a sudden shift once we cross that imagined line. We tend to view progress as a linear journey, like moving along a train track from one point to another.

However, the reality is that change and progress is a transition that is not always linear, and there is not always a distinct boundary between the before and after. Consistent progress is often subtle. Sometimes, we've already crossed that line without realizing it, and other times, progress occurs quietly in the background, even when it feels like nothing is happening. Sometimes while focusing on the progress of one thing, we forget that life continues on around it. Try to remain present and find a way to move through the process in a way that is enjoyable to you.

—— Tip 4

There Is No Line Between Here & There

Many of the small, seemingly insignificant steps we take daily contribute to the long-term, sustainable progress that eventually leads to the significant shifts we recognize as breakthroughs. Be patient through the transitions.

3

PROGRESSION THOUGH REFLECTION

— Tip 5

It All Begins With You

In the game of chess, the highest accolade a player can obtain is the title of Grandmaster. Once bestowed, this title is held for a lifetime. While a select number of Grandmasters exist worldwide, they epitomize excellence. I share this insight to emphasize that everything you desire originates with you. Much like a chess Grandmaster, you hold the status of Grandmaster in your life and in the art of manifesting. You wield the power to determine which pieces enter the game, how they're positioned, and how you navigate challenges. Though you may not be able to control everything, you **can** control how you react. Just as a Grandmaster shapes the outcome of a chess match, you mold the trajectory of your life.

Humans are reservoirs of immense power. Our gift of freewill isn't coincidental; it empowers us to create, transform, and influence energy. As you embark on this journey and engage with this book, I hope you know how powerful you really are in taking agency for your life. It all commences with you. You are the Grandmaster of Manifestation in your own life.

When we go looking too hard for the answer or get lost in the little details, we miss the big picture. Often in our excitement, we tend to try to predict everything that is coming in hopes to gain stability, clarity or control. We want all the answers and when we don't have them, we panic or hyper fixate. Any answers you seek will come exactly when you need them. Trust the process and trust yourself to gain clarity. But also learn to find the joy in not having all the answers. Sometimes the universe delivers beautiful surprises in the most unexpected of ways and we are gifted with better then we could ever imagine.

— Tip 6

Find Joy In Not Having All The Answers

— Tip 7

Shame Is Not A Productive Motivator

Be Curious Not Judemental

As you move through this journal, focus on observing yourself without judgment. Shame can block deep self-reflection and hinder the awareness needed for growth, while also reinforcing feelings of unworthiness. Instead, be gentle and approach yourself with curiosity and compassion.

It's okay to acknowledge your strengths while noticing areas for improvement. Growth is possible without harsh judgment—through self-awareness, unconditional self-love, and healthy support. You may also discover, as I did, that being hard on yourself often comes from lacking a clear way to track your progress. We tend to miss that which we don't acknowledge or pay attention to, especially when we are moving at a fast pace.

— Tip 8

Define What Success & Productivity Mean To You

One way to step away from society's hustle culture is to define success and productivity on your own terms. Consider what it means, feels and looks like for yourself based on the values and priorities you will outline in this journal. Give yourself permission to live life by your own terms.

FIRST MONTHLY CHECK IN:

DATE: / /

Let's get a sense of where you are and where you want to be...

HOW ARE YOU FEELING & WHAT IS CONTRIBUTING TO THESE FEELINGS...

PHYSICALLY:

EMOTIONALLY:

MENTALLY:

SPIRITUALLY:

IN RELATIONSHIPS:

IN CAREER:

SOCIALLY:

FINANCIALLY:

5

PROGRESSION THOUGH REFLECTION

IF ANYTHING WERE POSSIBLE, AND NOTHING AND NOBODY STOOD IN YOUR WAY, AND YOU COULD HAVE AND BE ANYTHING YOU COULD EVER WANT, WHAT WOULD IT BE? WHAT DO YOU WANT?

If you find this question difficult to answer, think about what you don't want first and then write the opposite.

PHYSICALLY: **EMOTIONALLY:**   **MENTALLY:**   **SPIRITUALLY:**

IN RELATIONSHIPS: **IN CAREER:**   **SOCIALLY:**   **FINANCIALLY:**

AND HOW WOULD YOU WANT TO FEEL...

PHYSICALLY: **EMOTIONALLY:**   **MENTALLY:**   **SPIRITUALLY:**

IN RELATIONSHIPS: **IN CAREER:**   **SOCIALLY:**   **FINANCIALLY:**

LIST ANYTHING THAT IS NOT CURRENTLY SERVING YOU OR THE VERSION OF YOU THAT YOU DESIRE TO BE IN ANY OF THE LISTED AREAS.

_____

_____

_____

_____

_____

_____

IN GENERAL, WHAT MAKES YOU FEEL REGULATED, AT PEACE AND/OR JOYFUL...

PHYSICALLY: **EMOTIONALLY:**   **MENTALLY:**   **SPIRITUALLY:**

IN RELATIONSHIPS: **IN CAREER:**   **SOCIALLY:**   **FINANCIALLY:**

BASED ON EVERYTHING YOU HAVE WRITTEN SO FAR, SEE IF YOU CAN IDENTIFY THE ROOT ENERGIES OF YOUR NEEDS & DESIRES. WHAT DO YOU ACTUALLY VALUE AND PRIORITIZE OR WHAT DO YOU WANT TO VALUE/PRIORITIZE...

PHYSICALLY: **EMOTIONALLY:**   **MENTALLY:**   **SPIRITUALLY:**

PROGRESSION THOUGH REFLECTION

IN RELATIONSHIPS: **IN CAREER:**   **SOCIALLY:**   **FINANCIALLY:**

WHAT HABITS SUPPORT OR HINDER YOUR DESIRES, VALUES AND PRIORITIES...

PHYSICALLY: **EMOTIONALLY:**   **MENTALLY:**   **SPIRITUALLY:**

IN RELATIONSHIPS: **IN CAREER:**   **SOCIALLY:**   **FINANCIALLY:**

GOALS:

WITH THE ABOVE INFORMATION IN MIND, MAKE A LIST OF GOALS YOU WOULD LIKE TO ACCOMPLISH & WHY.

It may help to put your goal in this format: I want to accomplish_____ because _____.

FOR EACH OF THE GOALS YOU LISTED, WRITE ONE OR MORE STEP(S) YOU CAN TAKE TO BRING YOU CLOSER TO EACH GOAL.

NOW PICK ONLY 3 TASKS ABOVE TO FOCUS ON THIS WEEK BY MARKING THEM WITH A STAR, HIGHLIGHTING, OR NUMBERING THEM.

Choose the three tasks that feel most aligned with your journey right now—whether that's what you're most intuitively drawn to, most excited about or what feels highest in priority. If priority is important to you this week, try numbering them from 1 to 3, with 1 being the most important. Choosing only three tasks at one time will keep the path forward clear and focused while limiting feelings of overwhelm.

Remember, if you finish these three tasks before the week is over, you can always come back to this page and take the next step. Use the extra space below if you need more room to organize your tasks or want to tackle a second group of tasks after completing the first this week.

MAKE A LIST OF ANY HABITS YOU WOULD LIKE TO BUILD OR BREAK RIGHT NOW. THEN LIST HOW EACH WILL SUPPORT THE VERSION OF YOU THAT YOU DESIRE FOR YOURSELF. (It may help to put your habits in this format: I want to break/build_____habit, because _____.)

Check In Day:

DATE: / /

Take a moment to check in, connect with your body, and track your progression through reflection. Skip any sections that don't apply or that don't resonate. Answer each question by reflecting on your experiences, progress, and challenges since your last check-in. Note any changes or anything else that stands out to you.

Gratitude Practice:
List at least 3 things for which you are grateful and why.

_____

_____

_____

_____

Physical Check In:

HOW DO YOU FEEL PHYSICALLY RIGHT NOW?

IN WHAT WAYS CAN YOU SUPPORT OR HONOR YOUR BODY AT THIS TIME?

_____   _____

_____   _____

Emotional Check In:

HOW DO YOU FEEL EMOTIONALLY RIGHT NOW?

What is contributing to how you feel Emotionally?

_____

_____

LIST ANY REOCCURRING EMOTIONS YOU RECALL FEELING.

What might these reoccurring feelings be telling you or what can you learn from them?

_____

_____

WHAT ARE YOU DISAPPOINTED OR DISCONTENT WITH AND WHY?

_____

_____

_____

_____

_____

HOW CAN YOU RESOLVE, HEAL OR CHANGE WHAT YOU FEEL DISAPPOINTED OR DISCONTENT WITH? OR, HOW CAN YOU SUPPORT YOURSELF AT THIS TIME IF A RESOLUTION, CHANGE OR HEALING IS NOT POSSIBLE AT THIS TIME?

_____

_____

_____

_____

_____

WHAT BROUGHT YOU JOY, PEACE, CONTENTMENT AND/OR HAPPINESS?

WHAT DO YOU FEEL PROUD OF OR PROUD OF YOURSELF FOR?

_____

_____

_____

Mental Check In:

HOW DO YOU FEEL MENTALLY RIGHT NOW?

What is contributing to how you feel Mentally?

_____

_____

11

LIST ANY RECURRING THOUGHTS YOU RECALL HAVING.

_____

_____

_____

WHAT MIGHT THESE RECURRING THOUGHTS BE TELLING YOU? WHAT CAN YOU GLEAN FROM THEM?

_____

_____

_____

LIST ANY LIMITING BELIEFS OR LIMITING THOUGHTS YOU RECALL HAVING.

_____

_____

_____

HOW CAN YOU CHALLENGE OR REFRAME EACH OF THE ABOVE?

_____

_____

_____

**Spiritual Check In:**

HOW DO YOU FEEL SPIRITUALLY RIGHT NOW?

What is contributing to how you feel spiritually?

_____

_____

WHAT DRAINED YOUR ENERGY ?

_____

_____

_____

_____

WHAT GAVE YOU ENERGY ?

_____

_____

_____

_____

Did you feel fully grounded and present?   ◯ Yes   ◯ No

If yes, what contributed to this feeling?

_____

If no, how can you foster more presence and ground yourself?

_____

Did you honor your boundaries?   ◯ Yes   ◯ No

If no, how can you better honor your boundaries moving forward?

_____

Did you honor your values and priorities?   ◯ Yes   ◯ No

If yes, how? Was it in the way you expected and if not, how did it differ from your expectations?

_____

If no, what got in the way and how can you better honor your values and priorities moving forward?

_____

HOW DID YOU NUTURE YOURSELF?
(Food, rest, movement, connection, spiritual practice, grounding, creativity, play, fun, other.)

_____

IS THERE ANYTHING YOU NEED RIGHT NOW THAT YOU ARE NOT GIVING YOURSELF?

_____

_____

Check in with your goals & progress:

DID YOU TAKE ANY STEPS TOWARDS ANY OF YOUR GOALS OR DO ANYTHING SMALL THAT ALIGNS WITH THE BIGGER VISION YOU HAVE FOR YOURSELF ?   ◯ Yes ◯ No

If yes, how? If no, what got in the way and what can you do differently tomorrow?

_____

_____

_____

LIST ANY GOALS THAT NEED MORE ATTENTION:

_____

_____

PROGRESSION THOUGH REFLECTION

LIST A SMALL STEP YOU CAN TAKE TOMORROW TOWARDS EACH TO GET THE BALL ROLLING.

_____

_____

LOOK BACK AT THE HABITS YOU ARE WORKING TO BUILD OR BREAK IN YOUR MONTHLY REFLECTION. HOW DID YOU DO? WHERE DID YOU SHOW DISCIPLINE AND WHERE DID YOU DEFAULT?

_____

_____

_____

_____

IF YOU DEFAULTED BACK TO A HABIT YOU ARE TRYING TO BREAK, HOW CAN YOU REINFORCE YOUR WHY AND/OR MOVE FORWARD IN A MORE ALIGNED WAY? IS THERE A SMALLER STEP YOU CAN TAKE FIRST THAT WOULD MAKE THE TRANSITION EASIER OR FEEL LEST RESISTANT?

_____

_____

_____

_____

DID YOU LEARN ANYTHING NEW ABOUT YOURSELF, YOUR GOALS, THE WAY YOU TRACK PROGRESS OR SOMETHING ELSE? IF SO, WRITE IT DOWN BELOW.

_____

_____

_____

_____

USE THE SPACE BELOW FOR ANY ADDITIONAL NOTES:

TAKE A MOMENT TO AFFIRM THE FOLLOWING:
I am exactly where I need to be right now. I fully accept myself as I am, where I am. I am capable, focused, and moving forward with purpose. I celebrate today's wins and welcome tomorrow's opportunities. I release judgment. I am worthy of everything I desire.

Check In Day:

DATE: /   /

Take a moment to check in, connect with your body, and track your progression through reflection. Skip any sections that don't apply or that don't resonate. Answer each question by reflecting on your experiences, progress, and challenges since your last check-in. Note any changes or anything else that stands out to you.

Gratitude Practice:

List at least 3 things for which you are grateful and why.

_____

_____

_____

_____

Physical Check In:

HOW DO YOU FEEL PHYSICALLY RIGHT NOW?

IN WHAT WAYS CAN YOU SUPPORT OR HONOR YOUR BODY AT THIS TIME?

_____   _____

_____   _____

Emotional Check In:

HOW DO YOU FEEL EMOTIONALLY RIGHT NOW?

What is contributing to how you feel Emotionally?

_____

_____

LIST ANY REOCCURRING EMOTIONS YOU RECALL FEELING.

What might these reoccurring feelings be telling you or what can you learn from them?

_____

_____

WHAT ARE YOU DISAPPOINTED OR DISCONTENT WITH AND WHY?

_____

_____

_____

_____

HOW CAN YOU RESOLVE, HEAL OR CHANGE WHAT YOU FEEL DISAPPOINTED OR DISCONTENT WITH? OR, HOW CAN YOU SUPPORT YOURSELF AT THIS TIME IF A RESOLUTION,CHANGE OR HEALING IS NOT POSSIBLE AT THIS TIME?

_____

_____

_____

_____

_____

WHAT BROUGHT YOU JOY, PEACE, CONTENTMENT AND/OR HAPPINESS?

WHAT DO YOU FEEL PROUD OF OR PROUD OF YOURSELF FOR?

_____

_____

_____

Mental Check In:

> ## HOW DO YOU FEEL MENTALLY RIGHT NOW?

What is contributing to how you feel Mentally?

_____

_____

LIST ANY RECURRING THOUGHTS YOU RECALL HAVING.

_____

_____

_____

WHAT MIGHT THESE RECURRING THOUGHTS BE TELLING YOU? WHAT CAN YOU GLEAN FROM THEM?

_____

_____

_____

LIST ANY LIMITING BELIEFS OR LIMITING THOUGHTS YOU RECALL HAVING.

_____

_____

_____

HOW CAN YOU CHALLENGE OR REFRAME EACH OF THE ABOVE?

_____

_____

_____

Spiritual Check In:

HOW DO YOU FEEL SPIRITUALLY RIGHT NOW?

What is contributing to how you feel spiritually?

_____

_____

PROGRESSION THOUGH REFLECTION

WHAT DRAINED YOUR ENERGY ?

_____

_____

_____

_____

WHAT GAVE YOU ENERGY ?

_____

_____

_____

_____

Did you feel fully grounded and present?   ○ Yes   ○ No

If yes, what contributed to this feeling?

_____

If no, how can you foster more presence and ground yourself?

_____

Did you honor your boundaries?   ○ Yes   ○ No

If no, how can you better honor your boundaries moving forward?

_____

Did you honor your values and priorities?   ○ Yes   ○ No

If yes, how? Was it in the way you expected and if not, how did it differ from your expectations?

_____

If no, what got in the way and how can you better honor your values and priorities moving forward?

_____

HOW DID YOU NUTURE YOURSELF?
(Food, rest, movement, connection, spiritual practice, grounding, creativity, play, fun, other.)

_____

IS THERE ANYTHING YOU NEED RIGHT NOW THAT YOU ARE NOT GIVING YOURSELF?

_____

_____

Check in with your goals & progress:

DID YOU TAKE ANY STEPS TOWARDS ANY OF YOUR GOALS OR DO ANYTHING SMALL THAT ALIGNS WITH THE BIGGER VISION YOU HAVE FOR YOURSELF ?   ○ Yes   ○ No

If yes, how? If no, what got in the way and what can you do differently tomorrow?

_____

_____

_____

LIST ANY GOALS THAT NEED MORE ATTENTION:

_____

_____

LIST A SMALL STEP YOU CAN TAKE TOMORROW TOWARDS EACH TO GET THE BALL ROLLING.

_____

_____

LOOK BACK AT THE HABITS YOU ARE WORKING TO BUILD OR BREAK IN YOUR MONTHLY REFLECTION. HOW DID YOU DO? WHERE DID YOU SHOW DISCIPLINE AND WHERE DID YOU DEFAULT?

_____

_____

_____

_____

IF YOU DEFAULTED BACK TO A HABIT YOU ARE TRYING TO BREAK, HOW CAN YOU REINFORCE YOUR WHY AND/OR MOVE FORWARD IN A MORE ALIGNED WAY? IS THERE A SMALLER STEP YOU CAN TAKE FIRST THAT WOULD MAKE THE TRANSITION EASIER OR FEEL LEST RESISTANT?

_____

_____

_____

_____

DID YOU LEARN ANYTHING NEW ABOUT YOURSELF, YOUR GOALS, THE WAY YOU TRACK PROGRESS OR SOMETHING ELSE? IF SO, WRITE IT DOWN BELOW.

_____

_____

_____

_____

USE THE SPACE BELOW FOR ANY ADDITIONAL NOTES:

TAKE A MOMENT TO AFFIRM THE FOLLOWING:
I am exactly where I need to be right now. I fully accept myself as I am, where I am. I am capable, focused, and moving forward with purpose. I celebrate today's wins and welcome tomorrow's opportunities. I release judgment. I am worthy of everything I desire.

Check In Day:

DATE: /   /

Take a moment to check in, connect with your body, and track your progression through reflection. Skip any sections that don't apply or that don't resonate. Answer each question by reflecting on your experiences, progress, and challenges since your last check-in. Note any changes or anything else that stands out to you.

Gratitude Practice:
List at least 3 things for which you are grateful and why.

_____

_____

_____

_____

Physical Check In:

HOW DO YOU FEEL PHYSICALLY RIGHT NOW?

IN WHAT WAYS CAN YOU SUPPORT OR HONOR YOUR BODY AT THIS TIME?

_____   _____

_____   _____

Emotional Check In:

HOW DO YOU FEEL EMOTIONALLY RIGHT NOW?

What is contributing to how you feel Emotionaliy?

_____

_____

LIST ANY REOCCURRING EMOTIONS YOU RECALL FEELING.

What might these reoccurring feelings be telling you or what can you learn from them?

_____

_____

WHAT ARE YOU DISAPPOINTED OR DISCONTENT WITH AND WHY?

_____

_____

_____

_____

_____

HOW CAN YOU RESOLVE, HEAL OR CHANGE WHAT YOU FEEL DISAPPOINTED OR DISCONTENT WITH? OR, HOW CAN YOU SUPPORT YOURSELF AT THIS TIME IF A RESOLUTION,CHANGE OR HEALING IS NOT POSSIBLE AT THIS TIME?

_____

_____

_____

_____

_____

WHAT BROUGHT YOU JOY, PEACE, CONTENTMENT AND/OR HAPPINESS?

WHAT DO YOU FEEL PROUD OF OR PROUD OF YOURSELF FOR?

_____

_____

_____

Mental Check In:

HOW DO YOU FEEL MENTALLY RIGHT NOW?

What is contributing to how you feel Mentally?

_____

_____

LIST ANY RECURRING THOUGHTS YOU RECALL HAVING.

_____

_____

_____

WHAT MIGHT THESE RECURRING THOUGHTS BE TELLING YOU? WHAT CAN YOU GLEAN FROM THEM?

_____

_____

_____

LIST ANY LIMITING BELIEFS OR LIMITING THOUGHTS YOU RECALL HAVING.

_____

_____

_____

HOW CAN YOU CHALLENGE OR REFRAME EACH OF THE ABOVE?

_____

_____

_____

Spiritual Check In:

HOW DO YOU FEEL SPIRITUALLY RIGHT NOW?

What is contributing to how you feel spiritually?

_____

_____

WHAT DRAINED YOUR ENERGY ?

_____

_____

_____

_____

WHAT GAVE YOU ENERGY ?

_____

_____

_____

_____

Did you feel fully grounded and present?   ◯ Yes   ◯ No

If yes, what contributed to this feeling?

_____

If no, how can you foster more presence and ground yourself?

_____

Did you honor your boundaries?   ◯ Yes   ◯ No

If no, how can you better honor your boundaries moving forward?

_____

Did you honor your values and priorities?   ◯ Yes   ◯ No

If yes, how? Was it in the way you expected and if not, how did it differ from your expectations?

_____

If no, what got in the way and how can you better honor your values and priorities moving forward?

_____

HOW DID YOU NUTURE YOURSELF?
(Food, rest, movement, connection, spiritual practice, grounding, creativity, play, fun, other.)

_____

IS THERE ANYTHING YOU NEED RIGHT NOW THAT YOU ARE NOT GIVING YOURSELF?

_____

_____

Check in with your goals & progress:
DID YOU TAKE ANY STEPS TOWARDS ANY OF YOUR GOALS OR DO ANYTHING SMALL THAT ALIGNS WITH THE BIGGER VISION YOU HAVE FOR YOURSELF ?   ◯ Yes ◯ No

If yes, how? If no, what got in the way and what can you do differently tomorrow?

_____

_____

_____

LIST ANY GOALS THAT NEED MORE ATTENTION:

_____

_____

PROGRESSION THOUGH REFLECTION

LIST A SMALL STEP YOU CAN TAKE TOMORROW TOWARDS EACH TO GET THE BALL ROLLING.

_____

_____

LOOK BACK AT THE HABITS YOU ARE WORKING TO BUILD OR BREAK IN YOUR MONTHLY REFLECTION. HOW DID YOU DO? WHERE DID YOU SHOW DISCIPLINE AND WHERE DID YOU DEFAULT?

_____

_____

_____

_____

IF YOU DEFAULTED BACK TO A HABIT YOU ARE TRYING TO BREAK, HOW CAN YOU REINFORCE YOUR WHY AND/OR MOVE FORWARD IN A MORE ALIGNED WAY? IS THERE A SMALLER STEP YOU CAN TAKE FIRST THAT WOULD MAKE THE TRANSITION EASIER OR FEEL LEST RESISTANT?

_____

_____

_____

_____

DID YOU LEARN ANYTHING NEW ABOUT YOURSELF, YOUR GOALS, THE WAY YOU TRACK PROGRESS OR SOMETHING ELSE? IF SO, WRITE IT DOWN BELOW.

_____

_____

_____

_____

USE THE SPACE BELOW FOR ANY ADDITIONAL NOTES:

TAKE A MOMENT TO AFFIRM THE FOLLOWING:
I am exactly where I need to be right now. I fully accept myself as I am, where I am. I am capable, focused, and moving forward with purpose. I celebrate today's wins and welcome tomorrow's opportunities. I release judgment. I am worthy of everything I desire.

FIRST WEEKLY CHECK IN:

DATE: / /

LIST ANY SYNCHRONICITIES YOU NOTICE FROM LAST WEEK'S REFLECTION OR IN YOUR LIFE IN GENERAL:

LIST ANY CHANGES OR ADJUSTMENTS YOU NEED TO MAKE & WHY:

GOALS:

WITH THE ABOVE & THE INFORMATION YOU WROTE IN YOUR MONTHLY SECTION IN MIND, MAKE A LIST OF GOALS YOU WOULD LIKE TO ACCOMPLISH & WHY.

It may help to put your goal in this format: I want to accomplish_____ because _____.

FOR EACH OF THE GOALS LISTED, WRITE ONE OR MORE STEP(S) YOU CAN TAKE TO BRING YOU CLOSER TO REACHING EACH GOAL.

NOW PICK ONLY 3 TASKS ABOVE TO FOCUS ON THIS WEEK BY MARKING THEM WITH A STAR, HIGHLIGHTING, OR NUMBERING THEM.

Choose the three tasks that feel most aligned with your journey right now—whether that's what you're most intuitively drawn to, most excited about or what feels highest in priority. If priority is important to you this week, try numbering them from 1 to 3, with 1 being the most important. Choosing only three tasks at one time will keep the path forward clear and focused while limiting feelings of overwhelm.

Remember, if you finish these three tasks before the week is over, you can always come back to this page and take the next step. Use the extra space below if you need more room to organize your tasks or want to tackle a second group of tasks after completing the first this week.

MAKE A LIST OF HABITS YOU WOULD LIKE TO BUILD OR BREAK RIGHT NOW. THEN LIST HOW EACH WILL SUPPORT THE VERSION OF YOU THAT YOU DESIRE FOR YOURSELF.

It may help to put your habits in this format: I want to break/build_____habit, because _____.

Check In Day:

DATE: / /

Take a moment to check in, connect with your body, and track your progression through reflection. Skip any sections that don't apply or that don't resonate. Answer each question by reflecting on your experiences, progress, and challenges since your last check-in. Note any changes or anything else that stands out to you.

Gratitude Practice:

List at least 3 things for which you are grateful and why.

_____

_____

_____

_____

Physical Check In:

HOW DO YOU FEEL PHYSICALLY RIGHT NOW?

IN WHAT WAYS CAN YOU SUPPORT OR HONOR YOUR BODY AT THIS TIME?

_____   _____

_____   _____

Emotional Check In:

HOW DO YOU FEEL EMOTIONALLY RIGHT NOW?

What is contributing to how you feel Emotionally?

_____

_____

LIST ANY REOCCURRING EMOTIONS YOU RECALL FEELING.

What might these reoccurring feelings be telling you or what can you learn from them?

_____

_____

WHAT ARE YOU DISAPPOINTED OR DISCONTENT WITH AND WHY?

_____

_____

_____

_____

_____

HOW CAN YOU RESOLVE, HEAL OR CHANGE WHAT YOU FEEL DISAPPOINTED OR DISCONTENT WITH? OR, HOW CAN YOU SUPPORT YOURSELF AT THIS TIME IF A RESOLUTION,CHANGE OR HEALING IS NOT POSSIBLE AT THIS TIME?

_____

_____

_____

_____

_____

WHAT BROUGHT YOU JOY, PEACE, CONTENTMENT AND/OR HAPPINESS?

WHAT DO YOU FEEL PROUD OF OR PROUD OF YOURSELF FOR?

_____

_____

_____

Mental Check In:

HOW DO YOU FEEL MENTALLY RIGHT NOW?

What is contributing to how you feel Mentally?

_____

_____

LIST ANY RECURRING THOUGHTS YOU RECALL HAVING.

_____

_____

_____

WHAT MIGHT THESE RECURRING THOUGHTS BE TELLING YOU? WHAT CAN YOU GLEAN FROM THEM?

_____

_____

_____

LIST ANY LIMITING BELIEFS OR LIMITING THOUGHTS YOU RECALL HAVING.

_____

_____

_____

HOW CAN YOU CHALLENGE OR REFRAME EACH OF THE ABOVE?

_____

_____

_____

Spiritual Check In:

HOW DO YOU FEEL SPIRITUALLY RIGHT NOW?

What is contributing to how you feel spiritually?

_____

_____

29

PROGRESSION THOUGH REFLECTION

WHAT DRAINED YOUR ENERGY ?

_____

_____

_____

_____

WHAT GAVE YOU ENERGY ?

_____

_____

_____

_____

Did you feel fully grounded and present?
If yes, what contributed to this feeling?

◯ Yes   ◯ No

If no, how can you foster more presence and ground yourself?

Did you honor your boundaries?
If no, how can you better honor your boundaries moving forward?

◯ Yes   ◯ No

Did you honor your values and priorities?
If yes, how? Was it in the way you expected and if not, how did it differ from your expectations?

◯ Yes   ◯ No

If no, what got in the way and how can you better honor your values and priorities moving forward?

HOW DID YOU NUTURE YOURSELF?
(Food, rest, movement, connection, spiritual practice, grounding, creativity, play, fun, other.)

IS THERE ANYTHING YOU NEED RIGHT NOW THAT YOU ARE NOT GIVING YOURSELF?

_____

_____

Check in with your goals & progress:

DID YOU TAKE ANY STEPS TOWARDS ANY OF YOUR GOALS OR DO ANYTHING SMALL THAT ALIGNS WITH THE BIGGER VISION YOU HAVE FOR YOURSELF ?   ◯ Yes   ◯ No
If yes, how? If no, what got in the way and what can you do differently tomorrow?

_____

_____

_____

LIST ANY GOALS THAT NEED MORE ATTENTION:

_____

_____

LIST A SMALL STEP YOU CAN TAKE TOMORROW TOWARDS EACH TO GET THE BALL ROLLING.

_____

_____

LOOK BACK AT THE HABITS YOU ARE WORKING TO BUILD OR BREAK IN YOUR WEEKLY REFLECTION. HOW DID YOU DO? WHERE DID YOU SHOW DISCIPLINE AND WHERE DID YOU DEFAULT?

_____

_____

_____

_____

IF YOU DEFAULTED BACK TO A HABIT YOU ARE TRYING TO BREAK, HOW CAN YOU REINFORCE YOUR WHY AND/OR MOVE FORWARD IN A MORE ALIGNED WAY? IS THERE A SMALLER STEP YOU CAN TAKE FIRST THAT WOULD MAKE THE TRANSITION EASIER OR FEEL LEST RESISTANT?

_____

_____

_____

_____

DID YOU LEARN ANYTHING NEW ABOUT YOURSELF, YOUR GOALS, THE WAY YOU TRACK PROGRESS OR SOMETHING ELSE? IF SO, WRITE IT DOWN BELOW.

_____

_____

_____

_____

USE THE SPACE BELOW FOR ANY ADDITIONAL NOTES:

TAKE A MOMENT TO AFFIRM THE FOLLOWING:
I am exactly where I need to be right now. I fully accept myself as I am, where I am. I am capable, focused, and moving forward with purpose. I celebrate today's wins and welcome tomorrow's opportunities. I release judgment. I am worthy of everything I desire.

Check In Day:

DATE: /   /

Take a moment to check in, connect with your body, and track your progression through reflection. Skip any sections that don't apply or that don't resonate. Answer each question by reflecting on your experiences, progress, and challenges since your last check-in. Note any changes or anything else that stands out to you.

Gratitude Practice:
List at least 3 things for which you are grateful and why.

_____

_____

_____

_____

Physical Check In:

| HOW DO YOU FEEL PHYSICALLY RIGHT NOW? | IN WHAT WAYS CAN YOU SUPPORT OR HONOR YOUR BODY AT THIS TIME? |

_____   _____

_____   _____

Emotional Check In:

HOW DO YOU FEEL EMOTIONALLY RIGHT NOW?

What is contributing to how you feel Emotionally?

_____

_____

LIST ANY REOCCURRING EMOTIONS YOU RECALL FEELING.

What might these reoccurring feelings be telling you or what can you learn from them?

_____

_____

WHAT ARE YOU DISAPPOINTED OR DISCONTENT WITH AND WHY?

_____

_____

_____

_____

_____

HOW CAN YOU RESOLVE, HEAL OR CHANGE WHAT YOU FEEL DISAPPOINTED OR DISCONTENT WITH? OR, HOW CAN YOU SUPPORT YOURSELF AT THIS TIME IF A RESOLUTION,CHANGE OR HEALING IS NOT POSSIBLE AT THIS TIME?

_____

_____

_____

_____

_____

WHAT BROUGHT YOU JOY, PEACE, CONTENTMENT AND/OR HAPPINESS?

WHAT DO YOU FEEL PROUD OF OR PROUD OF YOURSELF FOR?

_____

_____

_____

Mental Check In:

HOW DO YOU FEEL MENTALLY RIGHT NOW?

What is contributing to how you feel Mentally?

_____

_____

LIST ANY RECURRING THOUGHTS YOU RECALL HAVING.

_____

_____

_____

WHAT MIGHT THESE RECURRING THOUGHTS BE TELLING YOU? WHAT CAN YOU GLEAN FROM THEM?

_____

_____

_____

LIST ANY LIMITING BELIEFS OR LIMITING THOUGHTS YOU RECALL HAVING.

_____

_____

_____

HOW CAN YOU CHALLENGE OR REFRAME EACH OF THE ABOVE?

_____

_____

_____

Spiritual Check In:

HOW DO YOU FEEL SPIRITUALLY RIGHT NOW?

What is contributing to how you feel spiritually?

_____

_____

WHAT DRAINED YOUR ENERGY ?

_____
_____
_____
_____

WHAT GAVE YOU ENERGY ?

_____
_____
_____
_____

Did you feel fully grounded and present?   ◯ Yes   ◯ No

If yes, what contributed to this feeling?

_____

If no, how can you foster more presence and ground yourself?

_____

Did you honor your boundaries?   ◯ Yes   ◯ No

If no, how can you better honor your boundaries moving forward?

_____

Did you honor your values and priorities?   ◯ Yes   ◯ No

If yes, how? Was it in the way you expected and if not, how did it differ from your expectations?

_____

If no, what got in the way and how can you better honor your values and priorities moving forward?

_____

HOW DID YOU NUTURE YOURSELF?
(Food, rest, movement, connection, spiritual practice, grounding, creativity, play, fun, other.)

_____

IS THERE ANYTHING YOU NEED RIGHT NOW THAT YOU ARE NOT GIVING YOURSELF?

_____
_____

Check in with your goals & progress:

DID YOU TAKE ANY STEPS TOWARDS ANY OF YOUR GOALS OR DO ANYTHING SMALL THAT ALIGNS WITH THE BIGGER VISION YOU HAVE FOR YOURSELF ?   ◯ Yes   ◯ No

If yes, how? If no, what got in the way and what can you do differently tomorrow?

_____
_____

LIST ANY GOALS THAT NEED MORE ATTENTION:

_____
_____

PROGRESSION THOUGH REFLECTION

LIST A SMALL STEP YOU CAN TAKE TOMORROW TOWARDS EACH TO GET THE BALL ROLLING.

_____

_____

LOOK BACK AT THE HABITS YOU ARE WORKING TO BUILD OR BREAK IN YOUR WEEKLY REFLECTION. HOW DID YOU DO? WHERE DID YOU SHOW DISCIPLINE AND WHERE DID YOU DEFAULT?

_____

_____

_____

_____

IF YOU DEFAULTED BACK TO A HABIT YOU ARE TRYING TO BREAK, HOW CAN YOU REINFORCE YOUR WHY AND/OR MOVE FORWARD IN A MORE ALIGNED WAY? IS THERE A SMALLER STEP YOU CAN TAKE FIRST THAT WOULD MAKE THE TRANSITION EASIER OR FEEL LEST RESISTANT?

_____

_____

_____

_____

DID YOU LEARN ANYTHING NEW ABOUT YOURSELF, YOUR GOALS, THE WAY YOU TRACK PROGRESS OR SOMETHING ELSE? IF SO, WRITE IT DOWN BELOW.

_____

_____

_____

_____

USE THE SPACE BELOW FOR ANY ADDITIONAL NOTES:

TAKE A MOMENT TO AFFIRM THE FOLLOWING:
I am exactly where I need to be right now. I fully accept myself as I am, where I am. I am capable, focused, and moving forward with purpose. I celebrate today's wins and welcome tomorrow's opportunities. I release judgment. I am worthy of everything I desire.

Check In Day:

DATE: /   /

Take a moment to check in, connect with your body, and track your progression through reflection. Skip any sections that don't apply or that don't resonate. Answer each question by reflecting on your experiences, progress, and challenges since your last check-in. Note any changes or anything else that stands out to you.

Gratitude Practice:

List at least 3 things for which you are grateful and why.

_____

_____

_____

_____

Physical Check In:

HOW DO YOU FEEL PHYSICALLY RIGHT NOW?

IN WHAT WAYS CAN YOU SUPPORT OR HONOR YOUR BODY AT THIS TIME?

_____

_____

_____

_____

Emotional Check In:

HOW DO YOU FEEL EMOTIONALLY RIGHT NOW?

What is contributing to how you feel Emotionally?

_____

_____

LIST ANY REOCCURRING EMOTIONS YOU RECALL FEELING.

What might these reoccurring feelings be telling you or what can you learn from them?

_____

_____

PROGRESSION THOUGH REFLECTION

WHAT ARE YOU DISAPPOINTED OR DISCONTENT WITH AND WHY?

_____

_____

_____

_____

_____

HOW CAN YOU RESOLVE, HEAL OR CHANGE WHAT YOU FEEL DISAPPOINTED OR DISCONTENT WITH? OR, HOW CAN YOU SUPPORT YOURSELF AT THIS TIME IF A RESOLUTION,CHANGE OR HEALING IS NOT POSSIBLE AT THIS TIME?

_____

_____

_____

_____

_____

WHAT BROUGHT YOU JOY, PEACE, CONTENTMENT AND/OR HAPPINESS?

WHAT DO YOU FEEL PROUD OF OR PROUD OF YOURSELF FOR?

_____

_____

_____

Mental Check In:

HOW DO YOU FEEL MENTALLY RIGHT NOW?

What is contributing to how you feel Mentally?

_____

_____

LIST ANY RECURRING THOUGHTS YOU RECALL HAVING.

_____

_____

_____

WHAT MIGHT THESE RECURRING THOUGHTS BE TELLING YOU? WHAT CAN YOU GLEAN FROM THEM?

_____

_____

_____

LIST ANY LIMITING BELIEFS OR LIMITING THOUGHTS YOU RECALL HAVING.

_____

_____

_____

HOW CAN YOU CHALLENGE OR REFRAME EACH OF THE ABOVE?

_____

_____

_____

Spiritual Check In:

HOW DO YOU FEEL SPIRITUALLY RIGHT NOW?

What is contributing to how you feel spiritually?

_____

_____

PROGRESSION THOUGH REFLECTION

WHAT DRAINED YOUR ENERGY ?

_____

_____

_____

_____

WHAT GAVE YOU ENERGY ?

_____

_____

_____

_____

Did you feel fully grounded and present?   ◯ Yes   ◯ No

If yes, what contributed to this feeling?

_____

If no, how can you foster more presence and ground yourself?

_____

Did you honor your boundaries?   ◯ Yes   ◯ No

If no, how can you better honor your boundaries moving forward?

_____

Did you honor your values and priorities?   ◯ Yes   ◯ No

If yes, how? Was it in the way you expected and if not, how did it differ from your expectations?

_____

If no, what got in the way and how can you better honor your values and priorities moving forward?

_____

HOW DID YOU NUTURE YOURSELF?
(Food, rest, movement, connection, spiritual practice, grounding, creativity, play, fun, other.)

_____

IS THERE ANYTHING YOU NEED RIGHT NOW THAT YOU ARE NOT GIVING YOURSELF?

_____

_____

Check in with your goals & progress:

**DID YOU TAKE ANY STEPS TOWARDS ANY OF YOUR GOALS OR DO ANYTHING SMALL
THAT ALIGNS WITH THE BIGGER VISION YOU HAVE FOR YOURSELF ?**   ◯ Yes   ◯ No

If yes, how? If no, what got in the way and what can you do differently tomorrow?

_____

_____

LIST ANY GOALS THAT NEED MORE ATTENTION:

_____

_____

LIST A SMALL STEP YOU CAN TAKE TOMORROW TOWARDS EACH TO GET THE BALL ROLLING.

_____

_____

LOOK BACK AT THE HABITS YOU ARE WORKING TO BUILD OR BREAK IN YOUR WEEKLY REFLECTION. HOW DID YOU DO? WHERE DID YOU SHOW DISCIPLINE AND WHERE DID YOU DEFAULT?

_____

_____

_____

_____

IF YOU DEFAULTED BACK TO A HABIT YOU ARE TRYING TO BREAK, HOW CAN YOU REINFORCE YOUR WHY AND/OR MOVE FORWARD IN A MORE ALIGNED WAY? IS THERE A SMALLER STEP YOU CAN TAKE FIRST THAT WOULD MAKE THE TRANSITION EASIER OR FEEL LEST RESISTANT?

_____

_____

_____

_____

DID YOU LEARN ANYTHING NEW ABOUT YOURSELF, YOUR GOALS, THE WAY YOU TRACK PROGRESS OR SOMETHING ELSE? IF SO, WRITE IT DOWN BELOW.

_____

_____

_____

_____

USE THE SPACE BELOW FOR ANY ADDITIONAL NOTES:

TAKE A MOMENT TO AFFIRM THE FOLLOWING:
I am exactly where I need to be right now. I fully accept myself as I am, where I am. I am capable, focused, and moving forward with purpose. I celebrate today's wins and welcome tomorrow's opportunities. I release judgment. I am worthy of everything I desire.

WEEKLY CHECK IN:

DATE: / /

LIST ANY SYNCHRONICITIES YOU NOTICE FROM LAST WEEK'S REFLECTION OR IN YOUR LIFE IN GENERAL:

LIST ANY CHANGES OR ADJUSTMENTS YOU NEED TO MAKE & WHY:

GOALS:

WITH THE ABOVE & THE INFORMATION YOU WROTE IN YOUR MONTHLY SECTION IN MIND, MAKE A LIST OF GOALS YOU WOULD LIKE TO ACCOMPLISH & WHY.

It may help to put your goal in this format: I want to accomplish_____ because _____.

PROGRESSION THOUGH REFLECTION

FOR EACH OF THE GOALS LISTED, WRITE ONE OR MORE STEP(S) YOU CAN TAKE TO BRING YOU CLOSER TO REACHING EACH GOAL.

NOW PICK ONLY 3 TASKS ABOVE TO FOCUS ON THIS WEEK BY MARKING THEM WITH A STAR, HIGHLIGHTING, OR NUMBERING THEM.

Choose the three tasks that feel most aligned with your journey right now—whether that's what you're most intuitively drawn to, most excited about or what feels highest in priority. If priority is important to you this week, try numbering them from 1 to 3, with 1 being the most important. Choosing only three tasks at one time will keep the path forward clear and focused while limiting feelings of overwhelm.

Remember, if you finish these three tasks before the week is over, you can always come back to this page and take the next step. Use the extra space below if you need more room to organize your tasks or want to tackle a second group of tasks after completing the first this week.

MAKE A LIST OF HABITS YOU WOULD LIKE TO BUILD OR BREAK RIGHT NOW. THEN LIST HOW EACH WILL SUPPORT THE VERSION OF YOU THAT YOU DESIRE FOR YOURSELF.

It may help to put your habits in this format: I want to break/build_____habit, because _____.

Check In Day:

DATE: /   /

Take a moment to check in, connect with your body, and track your progression through reflection. Skip any sections that don't apply or that don't resonate. Answer each question by reflecting on your experiences, progress, and challenges since your last check-in. Note any changes or anything else that stands out to you.

Gratitude Practice:

List at least 3 things for which you are grateful and why.

_____

_____

_____

_____

Physical Check In:

HOW DO YOU FEEL PHYSICALLY RIGHT NOW?

IN WHAT WAYS CAN YOU SUPPORT OR HONOR YOUR BODY AT THIS TIME?

Emotional Check In:

HOW DO YOU FEEL EMOTIONALLY RIGHT NOW?

What is contributing to how you feel Emotionally?

LIST ANY REOCCURRING EMOTIONS YOU RECALL FEELING.

What might these reoccurring feelings be telling you or what can you learn from them?

WHAT ARE YOU DISAPPOINTED OR DISCONTENT WITH AND WHY?

_____

_____

_____

_____

_____

HOW CAN YOU RESOLVE, HEAL OR CHANGE WHAT YOU FEEL DISAPPOINTED OR DISCONTENT WITH? OR, HOW CAN YOU SUPPORT YOURSELF AT THIS TIME IF A RESOLUTION,CHANGE OR HEALING IS NOT POSSIBLE AT THIS TIME?

_____

_____

_____

_____

_____

WHAT BROUGHT YOU JOY, PEACE, CONTENTMENT AND/OR HAPPINESS?

WHAT DO YOU FEEL PROUD OF OR PROUD OF YOURSELF FOR?

_____

_____

_____

Mental Check In:

HOW DO YOU FEEL MENTALLY RIGHT NOW?

What is contributing to how you feel Mentally?

_____

_____

LIST ANY RECURRING THOUGHTS YOU RECALL HAVING.

_____

_____

_____

WHAT MIGHT THESE RECURRING THOUGHTS BE TELLING YOU? WHAT CAN YOU GLEAN FROM THEM?

_____

_____

_____

LIST ANY LIMITING BELIEFS OR LIMITING THOUGHTS YOU RECALL HAVING.

_____

_____

_____

HOW CAN YOU CHALLENGE OR REFRAME EACH OF THE ABOVE?

_____

_____

_____

Spiritual Check In:

HOW DO YOU FEEL SPIRITUALLY RIGHT NOW?

What is contributing to how you feel spiritually?

_____

_____

PROGRESSION THOUGH REFLECTION

WHAT DRAINED YOUR ENERGY ?

_____

_____

_____

_____

WHAT GAVE YOU ENERGY ?

_____

_____

_____

_____

Did you feel fully grounded and present?   ◯ Yes   ◯ No

If yes, what contributed to this feeling?

_____

If no, how can you foster more presence and ground yourself?

_____

Did you honor your boundaries?   ◯ Yes   ◯ No

If no, how can you better honor your boundaries moving forward?

_____

Did you honor your values and priorities?   ◯ Yes   ◯ No

If yes, how? Was it in the way you expected and if not, how did it differ from your expectations?

_____

If no, what got in the way and how can you better honor your values and priorities moving forward?

_____

HOW DID YOU NUTURE YOURSELF?
(Food, rest, movement, connection, spiritual practice, grounding, creativity, play, fun, other.)

_____

IS THERE ANYTHING YOU NEED RIGHT NOW THAT YOU ARE NOT GIVING YOURSELF?

_____

_____

Check in with your goals & progress:

DID YOU TAKE ANY STEPS TOWARDS ANY OF YOUR GOALS OR DO ANYTHING SMALL THAT ALIGNS WITH THE BIGGER VISION YOU HAVE FOR YOURSELF ?   ◯ Yes   ◯ No

If yes, how? If no, what got in the way and what can you do differently tomorrow?

_____

_____

LIST ANY GOALS THAT NEED MORE ATTENTION:

_____

_____

LIST A SMALL STEP YOU CAN TAKE TOMORROW TOWARDS EACH TO GET THE BALL ROLLING.

_____

_____

LOOK BACK AT THE HABITS YOU ARE WORKING TO BUILD OR BREAK IN YOUR WEEKLY REFLECTION. HOW DID YOU DO? WHERE DID YOU SHOW DISCIPLINE AND WHERE DID YOU DEFAULT?

_____

_____

_____

_____

IF YOU DEFAULTED BACK TO A HABIT YOU ARE TRYING TO BREAK, HOW CAN YOU REINFORCE YOUR WHY AND/OR MOVE FORWARD IN A MORE ALIGNED WAY? IS THERE A SMALLER STEP YOU CAN TAKE FIRST THAT WOULD MAKE THE TRANSITION EASIER OR FEEL LEST RESISTANT?

_____

_____

_____

_____

DID YOU LEARN ANYTHING NEW ABOUT YOURSELF, YOUR GOALS, THE WAY YOU TRACK PROGRESS OR SOMETHING ELSE? IF SO, WRITE IT DOWN BELOW.

_____

_____

_____

_____

USE THE SPACE BELOW FOR ANY ADDITIONAL NOTES:

TAKE A MOMENT TO AFFIRM THE FOLLOWING:
I am exactly where I need to be right now. I fully accept myself as I am, where I am. I am capable, focused, and moving forward with purpose. I celebrate today's wins and welcome tomorrow's opportunities. I release judgment. I am worthy of everything I desire.

Check In Day:

DATE: / /

Take a moment to check in, connect with your body, and track your progression through reflection. Skip any sections that don't apply or that don't resonate. Answer each question by reflecting on your experiences, progress, and challenges since your last check-in. Note any changes or anything else that stands out to you.

Gratitude Practice:

List at least 3 things for which you are grateful and why.

_____

_____

_____

_____

Physical Check In:

HOW DO YOU FEEL PHYSICALLY RIGHT NOW?

IN WHAT WAYS CAN YOU SUPPORT OR HONOR YOUR BODY AT THIS TIME?

_____   _____

_____   _____

Emotional Check In:

HOW DO YOU FEEL EMOTIONALLY RIGHT NOW?

What is contributing to how you feel Emotionally?

_____

_____

LIST ANY REOCCURRING EMOTIONS YOU RECALL FEELING.

What might these reoccurring feelings be telling you or what can you learn from them?

_____

_____

WHAT ARE YOU DISAPPOINTED OR DISCONTENT WITH AND WHY?

_____

_____

_____

_____

HOW CAN YOU RESOLVE, HEAL OR CHANGE WHAT YOU FEEL DISAPPOINTED OR DISCONTENT WITH? OR, HOW CAN YOU SUPPORT YOURSELF AT THIS TIME IF A RESOLUTION,CHANGE OR HEALING IS NOT POSSIBLE AT THIS TIME?

_____

_____

_____

_____

WHAT BROUGHT YOU JOY, PEACE, CONTENTMENT AND/OR HAPPINESS?

WHAT DO YOU FEEL PROUD OF OR PROUD OF YOURSELF FOR?

_____

_____

_____

Mental Check In:

HOW DO YOU FEEL MENTALLY RIGHT NOW?

What is contributing to how you feel Mentally?

_____

_____

LIST ANY RECURRING THOUGHTS YOU RECALL HAVING.

_____

_____

_____

WHAT MIGHT THESE RECURRING THOUGHTS BE TELLING YOU? WHAT CAN YOU GLEAN FROM THEM?

_____

_____

_____

LIST ANY LIMITING BELIEFS OR LIMITING THOUGHTS YOU RECALL HAVING.

_____

_____

_____

HOW CAN YOU CHALLENGE OR REFRAME EACH OF THE ABOVE?

_____

_____

_____

Spiritual Check In:

HOW DO YOU FEEL SPIRITUALLY RIGHT NOW?

What is contributing to how you feel spiritually?

_____

_____

WHAT DRAINED YOUR ENERGY ?

WHAT GAVE YOU ENERGY ?

_____

_____

_____

_____

Did you feel fully grounded and present?   ◯ Yes   ◯ No

If yes, what contributed to this feeling?

_____

If no, how can you foster more presence and ground yourself?

_____

Did you honor your boundaries?   ◯ Yes   ◯ No

If no, how can you better honor your boundaries moving forward?

_____

Did you honor your values and priorities?   ◯ Yes   ◯ No

If yes, how? Was it in the way you expected and if not, how did it differ from your expectations?

_____

If no, what got in the way and how can you better honor your values and priorities moving forward?

_____

HOW DID YOU NUTURE YOURSELF?
(Food, rest, movement, connection, spiritual practice, grounding, creativity, play, fun, other.)

_____

IS THERE ANYTHING YOU NEED RIGHT NOW THAT YOU ARE NOT GIVING YOURSELF?

_____

_____

Check in with your goals & progress:

**DID YOU TAKE ANY STEPS TOWARDS ANY OF YOUR GOALS OR DO ANYTHING SMALL
THAT ALIGNS WITH THE BIGGER VISION YOU HAVE FOR YOURSELF ?**   ◯ Yes ◯ No

If yes, how? If no, what got in the way and what can you do differently tomorrow?

_____

_____

LIST ANY GOALS THAT NEED MORE ATTENTION:

_____

_____

LIST A SMALL STEP YOU CAN TAKE TOMORROW TOWARDS EACH TO GET THE BALL ROLLING.

_____

_____

LOOK BACK AT THE HABITS YOU ARE WORKING TO BUILD OR BREAK IN YOUR WEEKLY REFLECTION. HOW DID YOU DO? WHERE DID YOU SHOW DISCIPLINE AND WHERE DID YOU DEFAULT?

_____

_____

_____

IF YOU DEFAULTED BACK TO A HABIT YOU ARE TRYING TO BREAK, HOW CAN YOU REINFORCE YOUR WHY AND/OR MOVE FORWARD IN A MORE ALIGNED WAY? IS THERE A SMALLER STEP YOU CAN TAKE FIRST THAT WOULD MAKE THE TRANSITION EASIER OR FEEL LEST RESISTANT?

_____

_____

_____

DID YOU LEARN ANYTHING NEW ABOUT YOURSELF, YOUR GOALS, THE WAY YOU TRACK PROGRESS OR SOMETHING ELSE? IF SO, WRITE IT DOWN BELOW.

_____

_____

_____

USE THE SPACE BELOW FOR ANY ADDITIONAL NOTES:

TAKE A MOMENT TO AFFIRM THE FOLLOWING:
I am exactly where I need to be right now. I fully accept myself as I am, where I am. I am capable, focused, and moving forward with purpose. I celebrate today's wins and welcome tomorrow's opportunities. I release judgment. I am worthy of everything I desire.

Check In Day:

DATE: /   /

Take a moment to check in, connect with your body, and track your progression through reflection. Skip any sections that don't apply or that don't resonate. Answer each question by reflecting on your experiences, progress, and challenges since your last check-in. Note any changes or anything else that stands out to you.

Gratitude Practice:
List at least 3 things for which you are grateful and why.

_____

_____

_____

_____

Physical Check In:

HOW DO YOU FEEL PHYSICALLY RIGHT NOW?

IN WHAT WAYS CAN YOU SUPPORT OR HONOR YOUR BODY AT THIS TIME?

_____   _____

_____   _____

Emotional Check In:

HOW DO YOU FEEL EMOTIONALLY RIGHT NOW?

What is contributing to how you feel Emotionally?

_____

_____

LIST ANY REOCCURRING EMOTIONS YOU RECALL FEELING.

What might these reoccurring feelings be telling you or what can you learn from them?

_____

_____

WHAT ARE YOU DISAPPOINTED OR DISCONTENT WITH AND WHY?

_____

_____

_____

_____

_____

HOW CAN YOU RESOLVE, HEAL OR CHANGE WHAT YOU FEEL DISAPPOINTED OR DISCONTENT WITH? OR, HOW CAN YOU SUPPORT YOURSELF AT THIS TIME IF A RESOLUTION,CHANGE OR HEALING IS NOT POSSIBLE AT THIS TIME?

_____

_____

_____

_____

_____

WHAT BROUGHT YOU JOY, PEACE, CONTENTMENT AND/OR HAPPINESS?

WHAT DO YOU FEEL PROUD OF OR PROUD OF YOURSELF FOR?

_____

_____

_____

Mental Check In:

HOW DO YOU FEEL MENTALLY RIGHT NOW?

What is contributing to how you feel Mentally?

_____

_____

LIST ANY RECURRING THOUGHTS YOU RECALL HAVING.

_____

_____

_____

WHAT MIGHT THESE RECURRING THOUGHTS BE TELLING YOU? WHAT CAN YOU GLEAN FROM THEM?

_____

_____

_____

LIST ANY LIMITING BELIEFS OR LIMITING THOUGHTS YOU RECALL HAVING.

_____

_____

_____

HOW CAN YOU CHALLENGE OR REFRAME EACH OF THE ABOVE?

_____

_____

_____

Spiritual Check In:

HOW DO YOU FEEL SPIRITUALLY RIGHT NOW?

What is contributing to how you feel spiritually?

_____

_____

PROGRESSION THOUGH REFLECTION

WHAT DRAINED YOUR ENERGY ?

_____

_____

_____

WHAT GAVE YOU ENERGY ?

_____

_____

_____

Did you feel fully grounded and present?   ◯ Yes   ◯ No

If yes, what contributed to this feeling?

If no, how can you foster more presence and ground yourself?

Did you honor your boundaries?   ◯ Yes   ◯ No

If no, how can you better honor your boundaries moving forward?

Did you honor your values and priorities?   ◯ Yes   ◯ No

If yes, how? Was it in the way you expected and if not, how did it differ from your expectations?

If no, what got in the way and how can you better honor your values and priorities moving forward?

HOW DID YOU NUTURE YOURSELF?
(Food, rest, movement, connection, spiritual practice, grounding, creativity, play, fun, other.)

IS THERE ANYTHING YOU NEED RIGHT NOW THAT YOU ARE NOT GIVING YOURSELF?

_____

_____

Check in with your goals & progress:

DID YOU TAKE ANY STEPS TOWARDS ANY OF YOUR GOALS OR DO ANYTHING SMALL THAT ALIGNS WITH THE BIGGER VISION YOU HAVE FOR YOURSELF ?   ◯ Yes   ◯ No

If yes, how? If no, what got in the way and what can you do differently tomorrow?

_____

_____

LIST ANY GOALS THAT NEED MORE ATTENTION:

_____

_____

LIST A SMALL STEP YOU CAN TAKE TOMORROW TOWARDS EACH TO GET THE BALL ROLLING.

_____

_____

LOOK BACK AT THE HABITS YOU ARE WORKING TO BUILD OR BREAK IN YOUR WEEKLY REFLECTION. HOW DID YOU DO? WHERE DID YOU SHOW DISCIPLINE AND WHERE DID YOU DEFAULT?

_____

_____

_____

_____

IF YOU DEFAULTED BACK TO A HABIT YOU ARE TRYING TO BREAK, HOW CAN YOU REINFORCE YOUR WHY AND/OR MOVE FORWARD IN A MORE ALIGNED WAY? IS THERE A SMALLER STEP YOU CAN TAKE FIRST THAT WOULD MAKE THE TRANSITION EASIER OR FEEL LEST RESISTANT?

_____

_____

_____

_____

DID YOU LEARN ANYTHING NEW ABOUT YOURSELF, YOUR GOALS, THE WAY YOU TRACK PROGRESS OR SOMETHING ELSE? IF SO, WRITE IT DOWN BELOW.

_____

_____

_____

_____

USE THE SPACE BELOW FOR ANY ADDITIONAL NOTES:

TAKE A MOMENT TO AFFIRM THE FOLLOWING:
I am exactly where I need to be right now. I fully accept myself as I am, where I am. I am capable, focused, and moving forward with purpose. I celebrate today's wins and welcome tomorrow's opportunities. I release judgment. I am worthy of everything I desire.

WEEKLY CHECK IN:

DATE: / /

LIST ANY SYNCHRONICITIES YOU NOTICE FROM LAST WEEK'S REFLECTION OR IN YOUR LIFE IN GENERAL:

LIST ANY CHANGES OR ADJUSTMENTS YOU NEED TO MAKE & WHY:

GOALS:

WITH THE ABOVE & THE INFORMATION YOU WROTE IN YOUR MONTHLY SECTION IN MIND, MAKE A LIST OF GOALS YOU WOULD LIKE TO ACCOMPLISH & WHY.

It may help to put your goal in this format: I want to accomplish_____ because _____.

FOR EACH OF THE GOALS LISTED, WRITE ONE OR MORE STEP(S) YOU CAN TAKE TO BRING YOU CLOSER TO REACHING EACH GOAL.

NOW PICK ONLY 3 TASKS ABOVE TO FOCUS ON THIS WEEK BY MARKING THEM WITH A STAR, HIGHLIGHTING, OR NUMBERING THEM.

Choose the three tasks that feel most aligned with your journey right now—whether that's what you're most intuitively drawn to, most excited about or what feels highest in priority. If priority is important to you this week, try numbering them from 1 to 3, with 1 being the most important. Choosing only three tasks at one time will keep the path forward clear and focused while limiting feelings of overwhelm.

Remember, if you finish these three tasks before the week is over, you can always come back to this page and take the next step. Use the extra space below if you need more room to organize your tasks or want to tackle a second group of tasks after completing the first this week.

MAKE A LIST OF HABITS YOU WOULD LIKE TO BUILD OR BREAK RIGHT NOW. THEN LIST HOW EACH WILL SUPPORT THE VERSION OF YOU THAT YOU DESIRE FOR YOURSELF.

It may help to put your habits in this format: I want to break/build_____habit, because _____.

Check In Day:

Take a moment to check in, connect with your body, and track your progression through reflection. Skip any sections that don't apply or that don't resonate. Answer each question by reflecting on your experiences, progress, and challenges since your last check-in. Note any changes or anything else that stands out to you.

Gratitude Practice:

List at least 3 things for which you are grateful and why.

_____

_____

_____

_____

Physical Check In:

HOW DO YOU FEEL PHYSICALLY RIGHT NOW?

IN WHAT WAYS CAN YOU SUPPORT OR HONOR YOUR BODY AT THIS TIME?

_____   _____

_____   _____

Emotional Check In:

HOW DO YOU FEEL EMOTIONALLY RIGHT NOW?

What is contributing to how you feel Emotionally?

_____

_____

LIST ANY REOCCURRING EMOTIONS YOU RECALL FEELING.

What might these reoccurring feelings be telling you or what can you learn from them?

_____

_____

PROGRESSION THOUGH REFLECTION

WHAT ARE YOU DISAPPOINTED OR DISCONTENT WITH AND WHY?

_____

_____

_____

_____

_____

HOW CAN YOU RESOLVE, HEAL OR CHANGE WHAT YOU FEEL DISAPPOINTED OR DISCONTENT WITH? OR, HOW CAN YOU SUPPORT YOURSELF AT THIS TIME IF A RESOLUTION,CHANGE OR HEALING IS NOT POSSIBLE AT THIS TIME?

_____

_____

_____

_____

_____

WHAT BROUGHT YOU JOY, PEACE, CONTENTMENT AND/OR HAPPINESS?

WHAT DO YOU FEEL PROUD OF OR PROUD OF YOURSELF FOR?

_____

_____

_____

Mental Check In:

HOW DO YOU FEEL MENTALLY RIGHT NOW?

What is contributing to how you feel Mentally?

_____

_____

LIST ANY RECURRING THOUGHTS YOU RECALL HAVING.

_____

_____

_____

WHAT MIGHT THESE RECURRING THOUGHTS BE TELLING YOU? WHAT CAN YOU GLEAN FROM THEM?

_____

_____

_____

LIST ANY LIMITING BELIEFS OR LIMITING THOUGHTS YOU RECALL HAVING.

_____

_____

_____

HOW CAN YOU CHALLENGE OR REFRAME EACH OF THE ABOVE?

_____

_____

_____

Spiritual Check In:

HOW DO YOU FEEL SPIRITUALLY RIGHT NOW?

What is contributing to how you feel spiritually?

_____

_____

PROGRESSION THOUGH REFLECTION

WHAT DRAINED YOUR ENERGY ?

_____

_____

_____

_____

WHAT GAVE YOU ENERGY ?

_____

_____

_____

_____

Did you feel fully grounded and present?   ◯ Yes   ◯ No

If yes, what contributed to this feeling?

_____

If no, how can you foster more presence and ground yourself?

_____

Did you honor your boundaries?   ◯ Yes   ◯ No

If no, how can you better honor your boundaries moving forward?

_____

Did you honor your values and priorities?   ◯ Yes   ◯ No

If yes, how? Was it in the way you expected and if not, how did it differ from your expectations?

_____

If no, what got in the way and how can you better honor your values and priorities moving forward?

_____

HOW DID YOU NUTURE YOURSELF?
(Food, rest, movement, connection, spiritual practice, grounding, creativity, play, fun, other.)

_____

IS THERE ANYTHING YOU NEED RIGHT NOW THAT YOU ARE NOT GIVING YOURSELF?

_____

_____

Check in with your goals & progress:

**DID YOU TAKE ANY STEPS TOWARDS ANY OF YOUR GOALS OR DO ANYTHING SMALL
THAT ALIGNS WITH THE BIGGER VISION YOU HAVE FOR YOURSELF ?**   ◯ Yes ◯ No

If yes, how? If no, what got in the way and what can you do differently tomorrow?

_____

_____

LIST ANY GOALS THAT NEED MORE ATTENTION:

_____

_____

LIST A SMALL STEP YOU CAN TAKE TOMORROW TOWARDS EACH TO GET THE BALL ROLLING.

_____

_____

LOOK BACK AT THE HABITS YOU ARE WORKING TO BUILD OR BREAK IN YOUR WEEKLY REFLECTION. HOW DID YOU DO? WHERE DID YOU SHOW DISCIPLINE AND WHERE DID YOU DEFAULT?

_____

_____

_____

IF YOU DEFAULTED BACK TO A HABIT YOU ARE TRYING TO BREAK, HOW CAN YOU REINFORCE YOUR WHY AND/OR MOVE FORWARD IN A MORE ALIGNED WAY? IS THERE A SMALLER STEP YOU CAN TAKE FIRST THAT WOULD MAKE THE TRANSITION EASIER OR FEEL LEST RESISTANT?

_____

_____

_____

_____

DID YOU LEARN ANYTHING NEW ABOUT YOURSELF, YOUR GOALS, THE WAY YOU TRACK PROGRESS OR SOMETHING ELSE? IF SO, WRITE IT DOWN BELOW.

_____

_____

_____

_____

USE THE SPACE BELOW FOR ANY ADDITIONAL NOTES:

TAKE A MOMENT TO AFFIRM THE FOLLOWING:
I am exactly where I need to be right now. I fully accept myself as I am, where I am. I am capable, focused, and moving forward with purpose. I celebrate today's wins and welcome tomorrow's opportunities. I release judgment. I am worthy of everything I desire.

Check In Day:

DATE: /   /

Take a moment to check in, connect with your body, and track your progression through reflection. Skip any sections that don't apply or that don't resonate. Answer each question by reflecting on your experiences, progress, and challenges since your last check-in. Note any changes or anything else that stands out to you.

Gratitude Practice:

List at least 3 things for which you are grateful and why.

_____

_____

_____

_____

Physical Check In:

HOW DO YOU FEEL PHYSICALLY RIGHT NOW?

IN WHAT WAYS CAN YOU SUPPORT OR HONOR YOUR BODY AT THIS TIME?

_____

_____

_____

_____

Emotional Check In:

HOW DO YOU FEEL EMOTIONALLY RIGHT NOW?

What is contributing to how you feel Emotionally?

_____

_____

LIST ANY REOCCURRING EMOTIONS YOU RECALL FEELING.

What might these reoccurring feelings be telling you or what can you learn from them?

_____

_____

WHAT ARE YOU DISAPPOINTED OR DISCONTENT WITH AND WHY?

_____

_____

_____

_____

_____

HOW CAN YOU RESOLVE, HEAL OR CHANGE WHAT YOU FEEL DISAPPOINTED OR DISCONTENT WITH? OR, HOW CAN YOU SUPPORT YOURSELF AT THIS TIME IF A RESOLUTION,CHANGE OR HEALING IS NOT POSSIBLE AT THIS TIME?

_____

_____

_____

_____

_____

WHAT BROUGHT YOU JOY, PEACE, CONTENTMENT AND/OR HAPPINESS?

WHAT DO YOU FEEL PROUD OF OR PROUD OF YOURSELF FOR?

_____

_____

_____

Mental Check In:

HOW DO YOU FEEL MENTALLY RIGHT NOW?

What is contributing to how you feel Mentally?

_____

_____

67

LIST ANY RECURRING THOUGHTS YOU RECALL HAVING.

_____

_____

_____

WHAT MIGHT THESE RECURRING THOUGHTS BE TELLING YOU? WHAT CAN YOU GLEAN FROM THEM?

_____

_____

_____

LIST ANY LIMITING BELIEFS OR LIMITING THOUGHTS YOU RECALL HAVING.

_____

_____

_____

HOW CAN YOU CHALLENGE OR REFRAME EACH OF THE ABOVE?

_____

_____

_____

Spiritual Check In:

HOW DO YOU FEEL SPIRITUALLY RIGHT NOW?

What is contributing to how you feel spiritually?

_____

_____

WHAT DRAINED YOUR ENERGY ?

_____

_____

_____

WHAT GAVE YOU ENERGY ?

_____

_____

_____

Did you feel fully grounded and present?   ◯ Yes   ◯ No

If yes, what contributed to this feeling?

If no, how can you foster more presence and ground yourself?

Did you honor your boundaries?   ◯ Yes   ◯ No

If no, how can you better honor your boundaries moving forward?

Did you honor your values and priorities?   ◯ Yes   ◯ No

If yes, how? Was it in the way you expected and if not, how did it differ from your expectations?

If no, what got in the way and how can you better honor your values and priorities moving forward?

HOW DID YOU NUTURE YOURSELF?
(Food, rest, movement, connection, spiritual practice, grounding, creativity, play, fun, other.)

IS THERE ANYTHING YOU NEED RIGHT NOW THAT YOU ARE NOT GIVING YOURSELF?

_____

_____

Check in with your goals & progress:

DID YOU TAKE ANY STEPS TOWARDS ANY OF YOUR GOALS OR DO ANYTHING SMALL THAT ALIGNS WITH THE BIGGER VISION YOU HAVE FOR YOURSELF ?   ◯ Yes   ◯ No

If yes, how? If no, what got in the way and what can you do differently tomorrow?

_____

_____

_____

LIST ANY GOALS THAT NEED MORE ATTENTION:

_____

_____

PROGRESSION THOUGH REFLECTION

LIST A SMALL STEP YOU CAN TAKE TOMORROW TOWARDS EACH TO GET THE BALL ROLLING.

_____

_____

LOOK BACK AT THE HABITS YOU ARE WORKING TO BUILD OR BREAK IN YOUR WEEKLY REFLECTION. HOW DID YOU DO? WHERE DID YOU SHOW DISCIPLINE AND WHERE DID YOU DEFAULT?

_____

_____

_____

_____

IF YOU DEFAULTED BACK TO A HABIT YOU ARE TRYING TO BREAK, HOW CAN YOU REINFORCE YOUR WHY AND/OR MOVE FORWARD IN A MORE ALIGNED WAY? IS THERE A SMALLER STEP YOU CAN TAKE FIRST THAT WOULD MAKE THE TRANSITION EASIER OR FEEL LEST RESISTANT?

_____

_____

_____

_____

DID YOU LEARN ANYTHING NEW ABOUT YOURSELF, YOUR GOALS, THE WAY YOU TRACK PROGRESS OR SOMETHING ELSE? IF SO, WRITE IT DOWN BELOW.

_____

_____

_____

_____

USE THE SPACE BELOW FOR ANY ADDITIONAL NOTES:

TAKE A MOMENT TO AFFIRM THE FOLLOWING:
I am exactly where I need to be right now. I fully accept myself as I am, where I am. I am capable, focused, and moving forward with purpose. I celebrate today's wins and welcome tomorrow's opportunities. I release judgment. I am worthy of everything I desire.

SECOND MONTHLY CHECK IN:

DATE: /   /

Let's get a sense of where you are and where you want to be...

HOW ARE YOU FEELING & WHAT IS CONTRIBUTING TO THESE FEELINGS...

PHYSICALLY:

EMOTIONALLY:

MENTALLY:

SPIRITUALLY:

IN RELATIONSHIPS:

IN CAREER:

SOCIALLY:

FINANCIALLY:

PROGRESSION THOUGH REFLECTION

IF ANYTHING WERE POSSIBLE, AND NOTHING AND NOBODY STOOD IN YOUR WAY, AND YOU COULD HAVE AND BE ANYTHING YOU COULD EVER WANT, WHAT WOULD IT BE? WHAT DO YOU WANT?

If you find this question difficult to answer, think about what you don't want first and then write the opposite.

PHYSICALLY:

EMOTIONALLY:

MENTALLY:

SPIRITUALLY:

IN RELATIONSHIPS:

IN CAREER:

SOCIALLY:

FINANCIALLY:

AND HOW WOULD YOU WANT TO FEEL...

PHYSICALLY:

EMOTIONALLY:

MENTALLY:

SPIRITUALLY:

IN RELATIONSHIPS:

IN CAREER:

SOCIALLY:

FINANCIALLY:

LIST ANYTHING THAT IS NOT CURRENTLY SERVING YOU OR THE VERSION OF YOU THAT YOU DESIRE TO BE IN ANY OF THE LISTED AREAS.

_____

_____

_____

_____

_____

_____

IN GENERAL, WHAT MAKES YOU FEEL REGULATED, AT PEACE AND/OR JOYFUL...

PHYSICALLY: EMOTIONALLY: MENTALLY: SPIRITUALLY:

IN RELATIONSHIPS: IN CAREER: SOCIALLY: FINANCIALLY:

BASED ON EVERYTHING YOU HAVE WRITTEN SO FAR, SEE IF YOU CAN IDENTIFY THE ROOT ENERGIES OF YOUR NEEDS & DESIRES. WHAT DO YOU ACTUALLY VALUE AND PRIORITIZE OR WHAT DO YOU WANT TO VALUE/PRIORITIZE...

PHYSICALLY: EMOTIONALLY: MENTALLY: SPIRITUALLY:

PROGRESSION THOUGH REFLECTION

IN RELATIONSHIPS: IN CAREER: SOCIALLY: FINANCIALLY:

WHAT HABITS SUPPORT OR HINDER YOUR DESIRES, VALUES AND PRIORITIES...

PHYSICALLY: EMOTIONALLY: MENTALLY: SPIRITUALLY:

IN RELATIONSHIPS: IN CAREER: SOCIALLY: FINANCIALLY:

GOALS:

WITH THE ABOVE INFORMATION IN MIND, MAKE A LIST OF GOALS YOU WOULD LIKE TO ACCOMPLISH & WHY.

It may help to put your goal in this format: I want to accomplish_____ because _____.

FOR EACH OF THE GOALS YOU LISTED, WRITE ONE OR MORE STEP(S) YOU CAN TAKE TO BRING YOU CLOSER TO EACH GOAL.

NOW PICK ONLY 3 TASKS ABOVE TO FOCUS ON THIS WEEK BY MARKING THEM WITH A STAR, HIGHLIGHTING, OR NUMBERING THEM.

Choose the three tasks that feel most aligned with your journey right now—whether that's what you're most intuitively drawn to, most excited about or what feels highest in priority. If priority is important to you this week, try numbering them from 1 to 3, with 1 being the most important. Choosing only three tasks at one time will keep the path forward clear and focused while limiting feelings of overwhelm.

Remember, if you finish these three tasks before the week is over, you can always come back to this page and take the next step. Use the extra space below if you need more room to organize your tasks or want to tackle a second group of tasks after completing the first this week.

MAKE A LIST OF ANY HABITS YOU WOULD LIKE TO BUILD OR BREAK RIGHT NOW. THEN LIST HOW EACH WILL SUPPORT THE VERSION OF YOU THAT YOU DESIRE FOR YOURSELF. (It may help to put your habits in this format: I want to break/build_____habit, because _____.)

Check In Day:

DATE: /   /

Take a moment to check in, connect with your body, and track your progression through reflection. Skip any sections that don't apply or that don't resonate. Answer each question by reflecting on your experiences, progress, and challenges since your last check-in. Note any changes or anything else that stands out to you.

Gratitude Practice:
List at least 3 things for which you are grateful and why.

_____

_____

_____

_____

Physical Check In:

HOW DO YOU FEEL PHYSICALLY RIGHT NOW?

IN WHAT WAYS CAN YOU SUPPORT OR HONOR YOUR BODY AT THIS TIME?

_____

_____

Emotional Check In:

HOW DO YOU FEEL EMOTIONALLY RIGHT NOW?

What is contributing to how you feel Emotionally?

_____

_____

LIST ANY REOCCURRING EMOTIONS YOU RECALL FEELING.

What might these reoccurring feelings be telling you or what can you learn from them?

_____

_____

WHAT ARE YOU DISAPPOINTED OR DISCONTENT WITH AND WHY?

_____

_____

_____

_____

_____

HOW CAN YOU RESOLVE, HEAL OR CHANGE WHAT YOU FEEL DISAPPOINTED OR DISCONTENT WITH? OR, HOW CAN YOU SUPPORT YOURSELF AT THIS TIME IF A RESOLUTION,CHANGE OR HEALING IS NOT POSSIBLE AT THIS TIME?

_____

_____

_____

_____

_____

WHAT BROUGHT YOU JOY, PEACE, CONTENTMENT AND/OR HAPPINESS?

WHAT DO YOU FEEL PROUD OF OR PROUD OF YOURSELF FOR?

_____

_____

_____

Mental Check In:

HOW DO YOU FEEL MENTALLY RIGHT NOW?

What is contributing to how you feel Mentally?

_____

_____

LIST ANY RECURRING THOUGHTS YOU RECALL HAVING.

_____

_____

_____

WHAT MIGHT THESE RECURRING THOUGHTS BE TELLING YOU? WHAT CAN YOU GLEAN FROM THEM?

_____

_____

_____

LIST ANY LIMITING BELIEFS OR LIMITING THOUGHTS YOU RECALL HAVING.

_____

_____

HOW CAN YOU CHALLENGE OR REFRAME EACH OF THE ABOVE?

_____

_____

_____

Spiritual Check In:

HOW DO YOU FEEL SPIRITUALLY RIGHT NOW?

What is contributing to how you feel spiritually?

_____

_____

WHAT DRAINED YOUR ENERGY ?

WHAT GAVE YOU ENERGY ?

Did you feel fully grounded and present?
If yes, what contributed to this feeling?

◯ Yes   ◯ No

If no, how can you foster more presence and ground yourself?

Did you honor your boundaries?
If no, how can you better honor your boundaries moving forward?

◯ Yes   ◯ No

Did you honor your values and priorities?
If yes, how? Was it in the way you expected and if not, how did it differ from your expectations?

◯ Yes   ◯ No

If no, what got in the way and how can you better honor your values and priorities moving forward?

HOW DID YOU NUTURE YOURSELF?
(Food, rest, movement, connection, spiritual practice, grounding, creativity, play, fun, other.)

IS THERE ANYTHING YOU NEED RIGHT NOW THAT YOU ARE NOT GIVING YOURSELF?

Check in with your goals & progress:

DID YOU TAKE ANY STEPS TOWARDS ANY OF YOUR GOALS OR DO ANYTHING SMALL THAT ALIGNS WITH THE BIGGER VISION YOU HAVE FOR YOURSELF ? ◯ Yes ◯ No
If yes, how? If no, what got in the way and what can you do differently tomorrow?

LIST ANY GOALS THAT NEED MORE ATTENTION:

PROGRESSION THOUGH REFLECTION

LIST A SMALL STEP YOU CAN TAKE TOMORROW TOWARDS EACH TO GET THE BALL ROLLING.

_____

_____

LOOK BACK AT THE HABITS YOU ARE WORKING TO BUILD OR BREAK IN YOUR MONTHLY REFLECTION. HOW DID YOU DO? WHERE DID YOU SHOW DISCIPLINE AND WHERE DID YOU DEFAULT?

_____

_____

_____

_____

IF YOU DEFAULTED BACK TO A HABIT YOU ARE TRYING TO BREAK, HOW CAN YOU REINFORCE YOUR WHY AND/OR MOVE FORWARD IN A MORE ALIGNED WAY? IS THERE A SMALLER STEP YOU CAN TAKE FIRST THAT WOULD MAKE THE TRANSITION EASIER OR FEEL LEST RESISTANT?

_____

_____

_____

_____

DID YOU LEARN ANYTHING NEW ABOUT YOURSELF, YOUR GOALS, THE WAY YOU TRACK PROGRESS OR SOMETHING ELSE? IF SO, WRITE IT DOWN BELOW.

_____

_____

_____

_____

USE THE SPACE BELOW FOR ANY ADDITIONAL NOTES:

TAKE A MOMENT TO AFFIRM THE FOLLOWING:
I am exactly where I need to be right now. I fully accept myself as I am, where I am. I am capable, focused, and moving forward with purpose. I celebrate today's wins and welcome tomorrow's opportunities. I release judgment. I am worthy of everything I desire.

Check In Day:

DATE: / /

Take a moment to check in, connect with your body, and track your progression through reflection. Skip any sections that don't apply or that don't resonate. Answer each question by reflecting on your experiences, progress, and challenges since your last check-in. Note any changes or anything else that stands out to you.

Gratitude Practice:

List at least 3 things for which you are grateful and why.

_____

_____

_____

_____

Physical Check In:

| HOW DO YOU FEEL PHYSICALLY RIGHT NOW? | IN WHAT WAYS CAN YOU SUPPORT OR HONOR YOUR BODY AT THIS TIME? |

_____

_____

Emotional Check In:

| HOW DO YOU FEEL EMOTIONALLY RIGHT NOW? | **What is contributing to how you feel Emotionally?** |

_____

_____

| LIST ANY REOCCURRING EMOTIONS YOU RECALL FEELING. | **What might these reoccurring feelings be telling you or what can you learn from them?** |

_____

_____

WHAT ARE YOU DISAPPOINTED OR DISCONTENT WITH AND WHY?

_____

_____

_____

_____

_____

HOW CAN YOU RESOLVE, HEAL OR CHANGE WHAT YOU FEEL DISAPPOINTED OR DISCONTENT WITH? OR, HOW CAN YOU SUPPORT YOURSELF AT THIS TIME IF A RESOLUTION,CHANGE OR HEALING IS NOT POSSIBLE AT THIS TIME?

_____

_____

_____

_____

_____

WHAT BROUGHT YOU JOY, PEACE, CONTENTMENT AND/OR HAPPINESS?

WHAT DO YOU FEEL PROUD OF OR PROUD OF YOURSELF FOR?

_____

_____

_____

Mental Check In:

| HOW DO YOU FEEL |
| MENTALLY RIGHT NOW? |

What is contributing to how you feel Mentally?

_____

_____

LIST ANY RECURRING THOUGHTS YOU RECALL HAVING.

_____

_____

_____

WHAT MIGHT THESE RECURRING THOUGHTS BE TELLING YOU? WHAT CAN YOU GLEAN FROM THEM?

_____

_____

_____

LIST ANY LIMITING BELIEFS OR LIMITING THOUGHTS YOU RECALL HAVING.

_____

_____

_____

HOW CAN YOU CHALLENGE OR REFRAME EACH OF THE ABOVE?

_____

_____

_____

Spiritual Check In:

HOW DO YOU FEEL SPIRITUALLY RIGHT NOW?

What is contributing to how you feel spiritually?

_____

_____

PROGRESSION THOUGH REFLECTION

WHAT DRAINED YOUR ENERGY ?

_____

_____

_____

_____

WHAT GAVE YOU ENERGY ?

_____

_____

_____

_____

Did you feel fully grounded and present?   ◯ Yes   ◯ No

If yes, what contributed to this feeling?

_____

If no, how can you foster more presence and ground yourself?

_____

Did you honor your boundaries?   ◯ Yes   ◯ No

If no, how can you better honor your boundaries moving forward?

_____

Did you honor your values and priorities?   ◯ Yes   ◯ No

If yes, how? Was it in the way you expected and if not, how did it differ from your expectations?

_____

If no, what got in the way and how can you better honor your values and priorities moving forward?

_____

HOW DID YOU NUTURE YOURSELF?
(Food, rest, movement, connection, spiritual practice, grounding, creativity, play, fun, other.)

_____

IS THERE ANYTHING YOU NEED RIGHT NOW THAT YOU ARE NOT GIVING YOURSELF?

_____

_____

Check in with your goals & progress:

DID YOU TAKE ANY STEPS TOWARDS ANY OF YOUR GOALS OR DO ANYTHING SMALL THAT ALIGNS WITH THE BIGGER VISION YOU HAVE FOR YOURSELF ?   ◯ Yes ◯ No

If yes, how? If no, what got in the way and what can you do differently tomorrow?

_____

_____

LIST ANY GOALS THAT NEED MORE ATTENTION:

_____

_____

LIST A SMALL STEP YOU CAN TAKE TOMORROW TOWARDS EACH TO GET THE BALL ROLLING.

_____

_____

LOOK BACK AT THE HABITS YOU ARE WORKING TO BUILD OR BREAK IN YOUR MONTHLY REFLECTION. HOW DID YOU DO? WHERE DID YOU SHOW DISCIPLINE AND WHERE DID YOU DEFAULT?

_____

_____

_____

_____

IF YOU DEFAULTED BACK TO A HABIT YOU ARE TRYING TO BREAK, HOW CAN YOU REINFORCE YOUR WHY AND/OR MOVE FORWARD IN A MORE ALIGNED WAY? IS THERE A SMALLER STEP YOU CAN TAKE FIRST THAT WOULD MAKE THE TRANSITION EASIER OR FEEL LEST RESISTANT?

_____

_____

_____

_____

DID YOU LEARN ANYTHING NEW ABOUT YOURSELF, YOUR GOALS, THE WAY YOU TRACK PROGRESS OR SOMETHING ELSE? IF SO, WRITE IT DOWN BELOW.

_____

_____

_____

_____

USE THE SPACE BELOW FOR ANY ADDITIONAL NOTES:

TAKE A MOMENT TO AFFIRM THE FOLLOWING:
I am exactly where I need to be right now. I fully accept myself as I am, where I am. I am capable, focused, and moving forward with purpose. I celebrate today's wins and welcome tomorrow's opportunities. I release judgment. I am worthy of everything I desire.

Check In Day:

DATE: /   /

Take a moment to check in, connect with your body, and track your progression through reflection. Skip any sections that don't apply or that don't resonate. Answer each question by reflecting on your experiences, progress, and challenges since your last check-in. Note any changes or anything else that stands out to you.

Gratitude Practice:
List at least 3 things for which you are grateful and why.

_____

_____

_____

_____

Physical Check In:

HOW DO YOU FEEL PHYSICALLY RIGHT NOW?

IN WHAT WAYS CAN YOU SUPPORT OR HONOR YOUR BODY AT THIS TIME?

_____

_____

Emotional Check In:

HOW DO YOU FEEL EMOTIONALLY RIGHT NOW?

What is contributing to how you feel Emotionally?

_____

_____

LIST ANY REOCCURRING EMOTIONS YOU RECALL FEELING.

What might these reoccurring feelings be telling you or what can you learn from them?

_____

_____

WHAT ARE YOU DISAPPOINTED OR DISCONTENT WITH AND WHY?

_____

_____

_____

_____

_____

HOW CAN YOU RESOLVE, HEAL OR CHANGE WHAT YOU FEEL DISAPPOINTED OR DISCONTENT WITH? OR, HOW CAN YOU SUPPORT YOURSELF AT THIS TIME IF A RESOLUTION,CHANGE OR HEALING IS NOT POSSIBLE AT THIS TIME?

_____

_____

_____

_____

_____

WHAT BROUGHT YOU JOY, PEACE, CONTENTMENT AND/OR HAPPINESS?

WHAT DO YOU FEEL PROUD OF OR PROUD OF YOURSELF FOR?

_____

_____

_____

Mental Check In:

HOW DO YOU FEEL MENTALLY RIGHT NOW?

What is contributing to how you feel Mentally?

_____

_____

LIST ANY RECURRING THOUGHTS YOU RECALL HAVING.

_____

_____

_____

WHAT MIGHT THESE RECURRING THOUGHTS BE TELLING YOU? WHAT CAN YOU GLEAN FROM THEM?

_____

_____

_____

LIST ANY LIMITING BELIEFS OR LIMITING THOUGHTS YOU RECALL HAVING.

_____

_____

_____

HOW CAN YOU CHALLENGE OR REFRAME EACH OF THE ABOVE?

_____

_____

_____

Spiritual Check In:

HOW DO YOU FEEL SPIRITUALLY RIGHT NOW?

What is contributing to how you feel spiritually?

_____

_____

WHAT DRAINED YOUR ENERGY ?

_____

_____

_____

_____

WHAT GAVE YOU ENERGY ?

_____

_____

_____

_____

Did you feel fully grounded and present?   ◯ Yes   ◯ No

If yes, what contributed to this feeling?

_____

If no, how can you foster more presence and ground yourself?

_____

Did you honor your boundaries?   ◯ Yes   ◯ No

If no, how can you better honor your boundaries moving forward?

_____

Did you honor your values and priorities?   ◯ Yes   ◯ No

If yes, how? Was it in the way you expected and if not, how did it differ from your expectations?

_____

If no, what got in the way and how can you better honor your values and priorities moving forward?

_____

HOW DID YOU NUTURE YOURSELF?
(Food, rest, movement, connection, spiritual practice, grounding, creativity, play, fun, other.)

_____

IS THERE ANYTHING YOU NEED RIGHT NOW THAT YOU ARE NOT GIVING YOURSELF?

_____

_____

Check in with your goals & progress:
DID YOU TAKE ANY STEPS TOWARDS ANY OF YOUR GOALS OR DO ANYTHING SMALL THAT ALIGNS WITH THE BIGGER VISION YOU HAVE FOR YOURSELF ?   ◯ Yes ◯ No

If yes, how? If no, what got in the way and what can you do differently tomorrow?

_____

_____

_____

LIST ANY GOALS THAT NEED MORE ATTENTION:

_____

_____

PROGRESSION THOUGH REFLECTION

LIST A SMALL STEP YOU CAN TAKE TOMORROW TOWARDS EACH TO GET THE BALL ROLLING.

_____

_____

LOOK BACK AT THE HABITS YOU ARE WORKING TO BUILD OR BREAK IN YOUR MONTHLY REFLECTION. HOW DID YOU DO? WHERE DID YOU SHOW DISCIPLINE AND WHERE DID YOU DEFAULT?

_____

_____

_____

_____

IF YOU DEFAULTED BACK TO A HABIT YOU ARE TRYING TO BREAK, HOW CAN YOU REINFORCE YOUR WHY AND/OR MOVE FORWARD IN A MORE ALIGNED WAY? IS THERE A SMALLER STEP YOU CAN TAKE FIRST THAT WOULD MAKE THE TRANSITION EASIER OR FEEL LEST RESISTANT?

_____

_____

_____

_____

DID YOU LEARN ANYTHING NEW ABOUT YOURSELF, YOUR GOALS, THE WAY YOU TRACK PROGRESS OR SOMETHING ELSE? IF SO, WRITE IT DOWN BELOW.

_____

_____

_____

_____

USE THE SPACE BELOW FOR ANY ADDITIONAL NOTES:

TAKE A MOMENT TO AFFIRM THE FOLLOWING:
I am exactly where I need to be right now. I fully accept myself as I am, where I am. I am capable, focused, and moving forward with purpose. I celebrate today's wins and welcome tomorrow's opportunities. I release judgment. I am worthy of everything I desire.

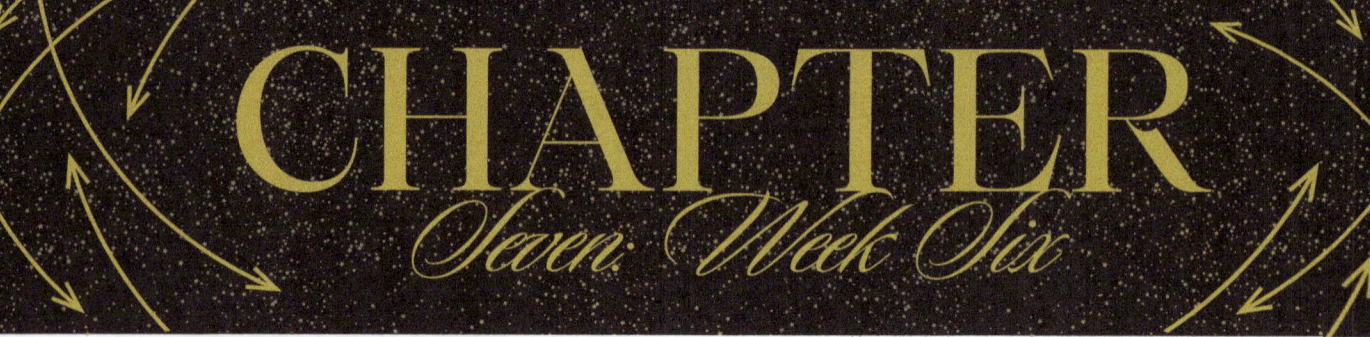

CHAPTER
Seven: Week Six

WEEKLY CHECK IN:

DATE: / /

LIST ANY SYNCHRONICITIES YOU NOTICE FROM LAST WEEK'S REFLECTION OR IN YOUR LIFE IN GENERAL:

LIST ANY CHANGES OR ADJUSTMENTS YOU NEED TO MAKE & WHY:

GOALS:

WITH THE ABOVE & THE INFORMATION YOU WROTE IN YOUR MONTHLY SECTION IN MIND, MAKE A LIST OF GOALS YOU WOULD LIKE TO ACCOMPLISH & WHY.

It may help to put your goal in this format: I want to accomplish_____ because _____.

FOR EACH OF THE GOALS LISTED, WRITE ONE OR MORE STEP(S) YOU CAN TAKE TO BRING YOU CLOSER TO REACHING EACH GOAL.

NOW PICK ONLY 3 TASKS ABOVE TO FOCUS ON THIS WEEK BY MARKING THEM WITH A STAR, HIGHLIGHTING, OR NUMBERING THEM.

Choose the three tasks that feel most aligned with your journey right now—whether that's what you're most intuitively drawn to, most excited about or what feels highest in priority. If priority is important to you this week, try numbering them from 1 to 3, with 1 being the most important. Choosing only three tasks at one time will keep the path forward clear and focused while limiting feelings of overwhelm.

Remember, if you finish these three tasks before the week is over, you can always come back to this page and take the next step. Use the extra space below if you need more room to organize your tasks or want to tackle a second group of tasks after completing the first this week.

MAKE A LIST OF HABITS YOU WOULD LIKE TO BUILD OR BREAK RIGHT NOW. THEN LIST HOW EACH WILL SUPPORT THE VERSION OF YOU THAT YOU DESIRE FOR YOURSELF.

It may help to put your habits in this format: I want to break/build_____habit, because _____.

Check In Day:

DATE: /   /

Take a moment to check in, connect with your body, and track your progression through reflection. Skip any sections that don't apply or that don't resonate. Answer each question by reflecting on your experiences, progress, and challenges since your last check-in. Note any changes or anything else that stands out to you.

Gratitude Practice:

List at least 3 things for which you are grateful and why.

_____

_____

_____

_____

Physical Check In:

HOW DO YOU FEEL PHYSICALLY RIGHT NOW?

IN WHAT WAYS CAN YOU SUPPORT OR HONOR YOUR BODY AT THIS TIME?

_____

_____

Emotional Check In:

HOW DO YOU FEEL EMOTIONALLY RIGHT NOW?

What is contributing to how you feel Emotionally?

_____

LIST ANY REOCCURRING EMOTIONS YOU RECALL FEELING.

What might these reoccurring feelings be telling you or what can you learn from them?

_____

WHAT ARE YOU DISAPPOINTED OR DISCONTENT WITH AND WHY?

_____

_____

_____

_____

_____

HOW CAN YOU RESOLVE, HEAL OR CHANGE WHAT YOU FEEL DISAPPOINTED OR DISCONTENT WITH? OR, HOW CAN YOU SUPPORT YOURSELF AT THIS TIME IF A RESOLUTION,CHANGE OR HEALING IS NOT POSSIBLE AT THIS TIME?

_____

_____

_____

_____

_____

WHAT BROUGHT YOU JOY, PEACE, CONTENTMENT AND/OR HAPPINESS?

WHAT DO YOU FEEL PROUD OF OR PROUD OF YOURSELF FOR?

_____

_____

_____

Mental Check In:

HOW DO YOU FEEL MENTALLY RIGHT NOW?

What is contributing to how you feel Mentally?

_____

_____

LIST ANY RECURRING THOUGHTS YOU RECALL HAVING.

_____

_____

_____

WHAT MIGHT THESE RECURRING THOUGHTS BE TELLING YOU? WHAT CAN YOU GLEAN FROM THEM?

_____

_____

_____

LIST ANY LIMITING BELIEFS OR LIMITING THOUGHTS YOU RECALL HAVING.

_____

_____

_____

HOW CAN YOU CHALLENGE OR REFRAME EACH OF THE ABOVE?

_____

_____

_____

Spiritual Check In:

HOW DO YOU FEEL SPIRITUALLY RIGHT NOW?

What is contributing to how you feel spiritually?

_____

_____

PROGRESSION THOUGH REFLECTION

WHAT DRAINED YOUR ENERGY ?

_____

_____

_____

_____

WHAT GAVE YOU ENERGY ?

_____

_____

_____

_____

Did you feel fully grounded and present?   ◯ Yes   ◯ No

If yes, what contributed to this feeling?

_____

If no, how can you foster more presence and ground yourself?

_____

Did you honor your boundaries?   ◯ Yes   ◯ No

If no, how can you better honor your boundaries moving forward?

_____

Did you honor your values and priorities?   ◯ Yes   ◯ No

If yes, how? Was it in the way you expected and if not, how did it differ from your expectations?

_____

If no, what got in the way and how can you better honor your values and priorities moving forward?

_____

HOW DID YOU NUTURE YOURSELF?
(Food, rest, movement, connection, spiritual practice, grounding, creativity, play, fun, other.)

_____

IS THERE ANYTHING YOU NEED RIGHT NOW THAT YOU ARE NOT GIVING YOURSELF?

_____

_____

Check in with your goals & progress:

**DID YOU TAKE ANY STEPS TOWARDS ANY OF YOUR GOALS OR DO ANYTHING SMALL
THAT ALIGNS WITH THE BIGGER VISION YOU HAVE FOR YOURSELF ?**   ◯ Yes   ◯ No

If yes, how? If no, what got in the way and what can you do differently tomorrow?

_____

_____

LIST ANY GOALS THAT NEED MORE ATTENTION:

_____

_____

LIST A SMALL STEP YOU CAN TAKE TOMORROW TOWARDS EACH TO GET THE BALL ROLLING.

_____

_____

LOOK BACK AT THE HABITS YOU ARE WORKING TO BUILD OR BREAK IN YOUR WEEKLY REFLECTION. HOW DID YOU DO? WHERE DID YOU SHOW DISCIPLINE AND WHERE DID YOU DEFAULT?

_____

_____

_____

_____

IF YOU DEFAULTED BACK TO A HABIT YOU ARE TRYING TO BREAK, HOW CAN YOU REINFORCE YOUR WHY AND/OR MOVE FORWARD IN A MORE ALIGNED WAY? IS THERE A SMALLER STEP YOU CAN TAKE FIRST THAT WOULD MAKE THE TRANSITION EASIER OR FEEL LEST RESISTANT?

_____

_____

_____

_____

DID YOU LEARN ANYTHING NEW ABOUT YOURSELF, YOUR GOALS, THE WAY YOU TRACK PROGRESS OR SOMETHING ELSE? IF SO, WRITE IT DOWN BELOW.

_____

_____

_____

_____

USE THE SPACE BELOW FOR ANY ADDITIONAL NOTES:

TAKE A MOMENT TO AFFIRM THE FOLLOWING:
I am exactly where I need to be right now. I fully accept myself as I am, where I am. I am capable, focused, and moving forward with purpose. I celebrate today's wins and welcome tomorrow's opportunities. I release judgment. I am worthy of everything I desire.

Check In Day:

Take a moment to check in, connect with your body, and track your progression through reflection. Skip any sections that don't apply or that don't resonate. Answer each question by reflecting on your experiences, progress, and challenges since your last check-in. Note any changes or anything else that stands out to you.

Gratitude Practice:

List at least 3 things for which you are grateful and why.

_____

_____

_____

_____

Physical Check In:

HOW DO YOU FEEL PHYSICALLY RIGHT NOW?

IN WHAT WAYS CAN YOU SUPPORT OR HONOR YOUR BODY AT THIS TIME?

_____

_____

Emotional Check In:

HOW DO YOU FEEL EMOTIONALLY RIGHT NOW?

What is contributing to how you feel Emotionally?

_____

_____

LIST ANY REOCCURRING EMOTIONS YOU RECALL FEELING.

What might these reoccurring feelings be telling you or what can you learn from them?

_____

_____

WHAT ARE YOU DISAPPOINTED OR DISCONTENT WITH AND WHY?

_____

_____

_____

_____

_____

HOW CAN YOU RESOLVE, HEAL OR CHANGE WHAT YOU FEEL DISAPPOINTED OR DISCONTENT WITH? OR, HOW CAN YOU SUPPORT YOURSELF AT THIS TIME IF A RESOLUTION,CHANGE OR HEALING IS NOT POSSIBLE AT THIS TIME?

_____

_____

_____

_____

_____

WHAT BROUGHT YOU JOY, PEACE, CONTENTMENT AND/OR HAPPINESS?

WHAT DO YOU FEEL PROUD OF OR PROUD OF YOURSELF FOR?

_____

_____

_____

Mental Check In:

HOW DO YOU FEEL
MENTALLY RIGHT NOW?

What is contributing to how you feel Mentally?

_____

_____

LIST ANY RECURRING THOUGHTS YOU RECALL HAVING.

_____

_____

_____

WHAT MIGHT THESE RECURRING THOUGHTS BE TELLING YOU? WHAT CAN YOU GLEAN FROM THEM?

_____

_____

_____

LIST ANY LIMITING BELIEFS OR LIMITING THOUGHTS YOU RECALL HAVING.

_____

_____

_____

HOW CAN YOU CHALLENGE OR REFRAME EACH OF THE ABOVE?

_____

_____

_____

Spiritual Check In:

HOW DO YOU FEEL SPIRITUALLY RIGHT NOW?

What is contributing to how you feel spiritually?

_____

_____

WHAT DRAINED YOUR ENERGY ?

_____

_____

_____

_____

WHAT GAVE YOU ENERGY ?

_____

_____

_____

_____

Did you feel fully grounded and present?   ◯ Yes   ◯ No

If yes, what contributed to this feeling?

_____

If no, how can you foster more presence and ground yourself?

_____

Did you honor your boundaries?   ◯ Yes   ◯ No

If no, how can you better honor your boundaries moving forward?

_____

Did you honor your values and priorities?   ◯ Yes   ◯ No

If yes, how? Was it in the way you expected and if not, how did it differ from your expectations?

_____

If no, what got in the way and how can you better honor your values and priorities moving forward?

_____

HOW DID YOU NUTURE YOURSELF?
(Food, rest, movement, connection, spiritual practice, grounding, creativity, play, fun, other.)

_____

IS THERE ANYTHING YOU NEED RIGHT NOW THAT YOU ARE NOT GIVING YOURSELF?

_____

_____

Check in with your goals & progress:
DID YOU TAKE ANY STEPS TOWARDS ANY OF YOUR GOALS OR DO ANYTHING SMALL THAT ALIGNS WITH THE BIGGER VISION YOU HAVE FOR YOURSELF ?   ◯ Yes   ◯ No

If yes, how? If no, what got in the way and what can you do differently tomorrow?

_____

_____

_____

LIST ANY GOALS THAT NEED MORE ATTENTION:

_____

_____

PROGRESSION THOUGH REFLECTION

LIST A SMALL STEP YOU CAN TAKE TOMORROW TOWARDS EACH TO GET THE BALL ROLLING.

_____

_____

LOOK BACK AT THE HABITS YOU ARE WORKING TO BUILD OR BREAK IN YOUR WEEKLY REFLECTION. HOW DID YOU DO? WHERE DID YOU SHOW DISCIPLINE AND WHERE DID YOU DEFAULT?

_____

_____

_____

IF YOU DEFAULTED BACK TO A HABIT YOU ARE TRYING TO BREAK, HOW CAN YOU REINFORCE YOUR WHY AND/OR MOVE FORWARD IN A MORE ALIGNED WAY? IS THERE A SMALLER STEP YOU CAN TAKE FIRST THAT WOULD MAKE THE TRANSITION EASIER OR FEEL LEST RESISTANT?

_____

_____

_____

DID YOU LEARN ANYTHING NEW ABOUT YOURSELF, YOUR GOALS, THE WAY YOU TRACK PROGRESS OR SOMETHING ELSE? IF SO, WRITE IT DOWN BELOW.

_____

_____

_____

USE THE SPACE BELOW FOR ANY ADDITIONAL NOTES:

TAKE A MOMENT TO AFFIRM THE FOLLOWING:
I am exactly where I need to be right now. I fully accept myself as I am, where I am. I am capable, focused, and moving forward with purpose. I celebrate today's wins and welcome tomorrow's opportunities. I release judgment. I am worthy of everything I desire.

Check In Day:

DATE: / /

Take a moment to check in, connect with your body, and track your progression through reflection. Skip any sections that don't apply or that don't resonate. Answer each question by reflecting on your experiences, progress, and challenges since your last check-in. Note any changes or anything else that stands out to you.

Gratitude Practice:

List at least 3 things for which you are grateful and why.

_____

_____

_____

_____

Physical Check In:

HOW DO YOU FEEL PHYSICALLY RIGHT NOW?

IN WHAT WAYS CAN YOU SUPPORT OR HONOR YOUR BODY AT THIS TIME?

_____

_____

Emotional Check In:

HOW DO YOU FEEL EMOTIONALLY RIGHT NOW?

What is contributing to how you feel Emotionally?

_____

_____

LIST ANY REOCCURRING EMOTIONS YOU RECALL FEELING.

What might these reoccurring feelings be telling you or what can you learn from them?

_____

_____

WHAT ARE YOU DISAPPOINTED OR DISCONTENT WITH AND WHY?

_____

_____

_____

_____

_____

HOW CAN YOU RESOLVE, HEAL OR CHANGE WHAT YOU FEEL DISAPPOINTED OR DISCONTENT WITH? OR, HOW CAN YOU SUPPORT YOURSELF AT THIS TIME IF A RESOLUTION,CHANGE OR HEALING IS NOT POSSIBLE AT THIS TIME?

_____

_____

_____

_____

_____

WHAT BROUGHT YOU JOY, PEACE, CONTENTMENT AND/OR HAPPINESS?

WHAT DO YOU FEEL PROUD OF OR PROUD OF YOURSELF FOR?

_____

_____

_____

Mental Check In:

HOW DO YOU FEEL MENTALLY RIGHT NOW?

What is contributing to how you feel Mentally?

_____

_____

LIST ANY RECURRING THOUGHTS YOU RECALL HAVING.

_____

_____

_____

WHAT MIGHT THESE RECURRING THOUGHTS BE TELLING YOU? WHAT CAN YOU GLEAN FROM THEM?

_____

_____

_____

LIST ANY LIMITING BELIEFS OR LIMITING THOUGHTS YOU RECALL HAVING.

_____

_____

_____

HOW CAN YOU CHALLENGE OR REFRAME EACH OF THE ABOVE?

_____

_____

_____

Spiritual Check In:

HOW DO YOU FEEL SPIRITUALLY RIGHT NOW?

What is contributing to how you feel spiritually?

_____

_____

PROGRESSION THOUGH REFLECTION

WHAT DRAINED YOUR ENERGY ?

_____

_____

_____

_____

WHAT GAVE YOU ENERGY ?

_____

_____

_____

_____

Did you feel fully grounded and present?   ◯ Yes   ◯ No

If yes, what contributed to this feeling?

_____

If no, how can you foster more presence and ground yourself?

_____

Did you honor your boundaries?   ◯ Yes   ◯ No

If no, how can you better honor your boundaries moving forward?

_____

Did you honor your values and priorities?   ◯ Yes   ◯ No

If yes, how? Was it in the way you expected and if not, how did it differ from your expectations?

_____

If no, what got in the way and how can you better honor your values and priorities moving forward?

_____

HOW DID YOU NUTURE YOURSELF?
(Food, rest, movement, connection, spiritual practice, grounding, creativity, play, fun, other.)

_____

IS THERE ANYTHING YOU NEED RIGHT NOW THAT YOU ARE NOT GIVING YOURSELF?

_____

_____

Check in with your goals & progress:

**DID YOU TAKE ANY STEPS TOWARDS ANY OF YOUR GOALS OR DO ANYTHING SMALL
THAT ALIGNS WITH THE BIGGER VISION YOU HAVE FOR YOURSELF ?**   ◯ Yes ◯ No

If yes, how? If no, what got in the way and what can you do differently tomorrow?

_____

_____

LIST ANY GOALS THAT NEED MORE ATTENTION:

_____

_____

LIST A SMALL STEP YOU CAN TAKE TOMORROW TOWARDS EACH TO GET THE BALL ROLLING.

_____

_____

LOOK BACK AT THE HABITS YOU ARE WORKING TO BUILD OR BREAK IN YOUR WEEKLY REFLECTION. HOW DID YOU DO? WHERE DID YOU SHOW DISCIPLINE AND WHERE DID YOU DEFAULT?

_____

_____

_____

_____

IF YOU DEFAULTED BACK TO A HABIT YOU ARE TRYING TO BREAK, HOW CAN YOU REINFORCE YOUR WHY AND/OR MOVE FORWARD IN A MORE ALIGNED WAY? IS THERE A SMALLER STEP YOU CAN TAKE FIRST THAT WOULD MAKE THE TRANSITION EASIER OR FEEL LEST RESISTANT?

_____

_____

_____

_____

DID YOU LEARN ANYTHING NEW ABOUT YOURSELF, YOUR GOALS, THE WAY YOU TRACK PROGRESS OR SOMETHING ELSE? IF SO, WRITE IT DOWN BELOW.

_____

_____

_____

_____

USE THE SPACE BELOW FOR ANY ADDITIONAL NOTES:

TAKE A MOMENT TO AFFIRM THE FOLLOWING:
I am exactly where I need to be right now. I fully accept myself as I am, where I am. I am capable, focused, and moving forward with purpose. I celebrate today's wins and welcome tomorrow's opportunities. I release judgment. I am worthy of everything I desire.

WEEKLY CHECK IN:

DATE: / /

LIST ANY SYNCHRONICITIES YOU NOTICE FROM LAST WEEK'S REFLECTION OR IN YOUR LIFE IN GENERAL:

LIST ANY CHANGES OR ADJUSTMENTS YOU NEED TO MAKE & WHY:

GOALS:

WITH THE ABOVE & THE INFORMATION YOU WROTE IN YOUR MONTHLY SECTION IN MIND, MAKE A LIST OF GOALS YOU WOULD LIKE TO ACCOMPLISH & WHY.

It may help to put your goal in this format: I want to accomplish_____ because _____.

FOR EACH OF THE GOALS LISTED, WRITE ONE OR MORE STEP(S) YOU CAN TAKE TO BRING YOU CLOSER TO REACHING EACH GOAL.

NOW PICK ONLY 3 TASKS ABOVE TO FOCUS ON THIS WEEK BY MARKING THEM WITH A STAR, HIGHLIGHTING, OR NUMBERING THEM.

Choose the three tasks that feel most aligned with your journey right now—whether that's what you're most intuitively drawn to, most excited about or what feels highest in priority. If priority is important to you this week, try numbering them from 1 to 3, with 1 being the most important. Choosing only three tasks at one time will keep the path forward clear and focused while limiting feelings of overwhelm.

Remember, if you finish these three tasks before the week is over, you can always come back to this page and take the next step. Use the extra space below if you need more room to organize your tasks or want to tackle a second group of tasks after completing the first this week.

MAKE A LIST OF HABITS YOU WOULD LIKE TO BUILD OR BREAK RIGHT NOW. THEN LIST HOW EACH WILL SUPPORT THE VERSION OF YOU THAT YOU DESIRE FOR YOURSELF.

It may help to put your habits in this format: I want to break/build_____habit, because _____.

Check In Day:

DATE: / /

Take a moment to check in, connect with your body, and track your progression through reflection. Skip any sections that don't apply or that don't resonate. Answer each question by reflecting on your experiences, progress, and challenges since your last check-in. Note any changes or anything else that stands out to you.

Gratitude Practice:
List at least 3 things for which you are grateful and why.

_____

_____

_____

_____

Physical Check In:

HOW DO YOU FEEL PHYSICALLY RIGHT NOW?

IN WHAT WAYS CAN YOU SUPPORT OR HONOR YOUR BODY AT THIS TIME?

_____

_____

Emotional Check In:

HOW DO YOU FEEL EMOTIONALLY RIGHT NOW?

What is contributing to how you feel Emotionally?

_____

LIST ANY REOCCURRING EMOTIONS YOU RECALL FEELING.

What might these reoccurring feelings be telling you or what can you learn from them?

_____

WHAT ARE YOU DISAPPOINTED OR DISCONTENT WITH AND WHY?

_____

_____

_____

_____

_____

HOW CAN YOU RESOLVE, HEAL OR CHANGE WHAT YOU FEEL DISAPPOINTED OR DISCONTENT WITH? OR, HOW CAN YOU SUPPORT YOURSELF AT THIS TIME IF A RESOLUTION,CHANGE OR HEALING IS NOT POSSIBLE AT THIS TIME?

_____

_____

_____

_____

_____

WHAT BROUGHT YOU JOY, PEACE, CONTENTMENT AND/OR HAPPINESS?

WHAT DO YOU FEEL PROUD OF OR PROUD OF YOURSELF FOR?

_____

_____

_____

Mental Check In:

HOW DO YOU FEEL MENTALLY RIGHT NOW?

What is contributing to how you feel Mentally?

_____

_____

LIST ANY RECURRING THOUGHTS YOU RECALL HAVING.

_____

_____

_____

WHAT MIGHT THESE RECURRING THOUGHTS BE TELLING YOU? WHAT CAN YOU GLEAN FROM THEM?

_____

_____

_____

LIST ANY LIMITING BELIEFS OR LIMITING THOUGHTS YOU RECALL HAVING.

_____

_____

_____

HOW CAN YOU CHALLENGE OR REFRAME EACH OF THE ABOVE?

_____

_____

_____

Spiritual Check In:

HOW DO YOU FEEL SPIRITUALLY RIGHT NOW?

What is contributing to how you feel spiritually?

_____

_____

PROGRESSION THOUGH REFLECTION

WHAT DRAINED YOUR ENERGY ?

_____

_____

_____

_____

WHAT GAVE YOU ENERGY ?

_____

_____

_____

_____

Did you feel fully grounded and present?   ◯ Yes   ◯ No

If yes, what contributed to this feeling?

_____

If no, how can you foster more presence and ground yourself?

_____

Did you honor your boundaries?   ◯ Yes   ◯ No

If no, how can you better honor your boundaries moving forward?

_____

Did you honor your values and priorities?   ◯ Yes   ◯ No

If yes, how? Was it in the way you expected and if not, how did it differ from your expectations?

_____

If no, what got in the way and how can you better honor your values and priorities moving forward?

_____

HOW DID YOU NUTURE YOURSELF?

(Food, rest, movement, connection, spiritual practice, grounding, creativity, play, fun, other.)

_____

IS THERE ANYTHING YOU NEED RIGHT NOW THAT YOU ARE NOT GIVING YOURSELF?

_____

_____

Check in with your goals & progress:

DID YOU TAKE ANY STEPS TOWARDS ANY OF YOUR GOALS OR DO ANYTHING SMALL THAT ALIGNS WITH THE BIGGER VISION YOU HAVE FOR YOURSELF ?   ◯ Yes   ◯ No

If yes, how? If no, what got in the way and what can you do differently tomorrow?

_____

_____

_____

LIST ANY GOALS THAT NEED MORE ATTENTION:

_____

_____

LIST A SMALL STEP YOU CAN TAKE TOMORROW TOWARDS EACH TO GET THE BALL ROLLING.

_____

_____

LOOK BACK AT THE HABITS YOU ARE WORKING TO BUILD OR BREAK IN YOUR WEEKLY REFLECTION. HOW DID YOU DO? WHERE DID YOU SHOW DISCIPLINE AND WHERE DID YOU DEFAULT?

_____

_____

_____

_____

IF YOU DEFAULTED BACK TO A HABIT YOU ARE TRYING TO BREAK, HOW CAN YOU REINFORCE YOUR WHY AND/OR MOVE FORWARD IN A MORE ALIGNED WAY? IS THERE A SMALLER STEP YOU CAN TAKE FIRST THAT WOULD MAKE THE TRANSITION EASIER OR FEEL LEST RESISTANT?

_____

_____

_____

_____

DID YOU LEARN ANYTHING NEW ABOUT YOURSELF, YOUR GOALS, THE WAY YOU TRACK PROGRESS OR SOMETHING ELSE? IF SO, WRITE IT DOWN BELOW.

_____

_____

_____

_____

USE THE SPACE BELOW FOR ANY ADDITIONAL NOTES:

TAKE A MOMENT TO AFFIRM THE FOLLOWING:
I am exactly where I need to be right now. I fully accept myself as I am, where I am. I am capable, focused, and moving forward with purpose. I celebrate today's wins and welcome tomorrow's opportunities. I release judgment. I am worthy of everything I desire.

Check In Day:

DATE: /   /

Take a moment to check in, connect with your body, and track your progression through reflection. Skip any sections that don't apply or that don't resonate. Answer each question by reflecting on your experiences, progress, and challenges since your last check-in. Note any changes or anything else that stands out to you.

Gratitude Practice:
List at least 3 things for which you are grateful and why.

_____

_____

_____

_____

Physical Check In:

| HOW DO YOU FEEL PHYSICALLY RIGHT NOW? | IN WHAT WAYS CAN YOU SUPPORT OR HONOR YOUR BODY AT THIS TIME? |

_____   _____

_____   _____

Emotional Check In:

| HOW DO YOU FEEL EMOTIONALLY RIGHT NOW? | **What is contributing to how you feel Emotionally?** |

_____

_____

| LIST ANY REOCCURRING EMOTIONS YOU RECALL FEELING. | **What might these reoccurring feelings be telling you or what can you learn from them?** |

_____

_____

115

WHAT ARE YOU DISAPPOINTED OR DISCONTENT WITH AND WHY?

_____

_____

_____

_____

_____

HOW CAN YOU RESOLVE, HEAL OR CHANGE WHAT YOU FEEL DISAPPOINTED OR DISCONTENT WITH? OR, HOW CAN YOU SUPPORT YOURSELF AT THIS TIME IF A RESOLUTION,CHANGE OR HEALING IS NOT POSSIBLE AT THIS TIME?

_____

_____

_____

_____

_____

WHAT BROUGHT YOU JOY, PEACE, CONTENTMENT AND/OR HAPPINESS?

WHAT DO YOU FEEL PROUD OF OR PROUD OF YOURSELF FOR?

_____

_____

_____

Mental Check In:

HOW DO YOU FEEL MENTALLY RIGHT NOW?

What is contributing to how you feel Mentally?

_____

_____

LIST ANY RECURRING THOUGHTS YOU RECALL HAVING.

_____

_____

_____

WHAT MIGHT THESE RECURRING THOUGHTS BE TELLING YOU? WHAT CAN YOU GLEAN FROM THEM?

_____

_____

_____

LIST ANY LIMITING BELIEFS OR LIMITING THOUGHTS YOU RECALL HAVING.

_____

_____

_____

HOW CAN YOU CHALLENGE OR REFRAME EACH OF THE ABOVE?

_____

_____

_____

Spiritual Check In:

HOW DO YOU FEEL SPIRITUALLY RIGHT NOW?

What is contributing to how you feel spiritually?

_____

_____

WHAT DRAINED YOUR ENERGY ?

_____

_____

_____

_____

WHAT GAVE YOU ENERGY ?

_____

_____

_____

_____

Did you feel fully grounded and present?   ◯ Yes   ◯ No

If yes, what contributed to this feeling?

_____

If no, how can you foster more presence and ground yourself?

_____

Did you honor your boundaries?   ◯ Yes   ◯ No

If no, how can you better honor your boundaries moving forward?

_____

Did you honor your values and priorities?   ◯ Yes   ◯ No

If yes, how? Was it in the way you expected and if not, how did it differ from your expectations?

_____

If no, what got in the way and how can you better honor your values and priorities moving forward?

_____

HOW DID YOU NUTURE YOURSELF?

(Food, rest, movement, connection, spiritual practice, grounding, creativity, play, fun, other.)

_____

IS THERE ANYTHING YOU NEED RIGHT NOW THAT YOU ARE NOT GIVING YOURSELF?

_____

_____

Check in with your goals & progress:

DID YOU TAKE ANY STEPS TOWARDS ANY OF YOUR GOALS OR DO ANYTHING SMALL THAT ALIGNS WITH THE BIGGER VISION YOU HAVE FOR YOURSELF ?   ◯ Yes ◯ No

If yes, how? If no, what got in the way and what can you do differently tomorrow?

_____

_____

_____

LIST ANY GOALS THAT NEED MORE ATTENTION:

_____

_____

PROGRESSION THOUGH REFLECTION

LIST A SMALL STEP YOU CAN TAKE TOMORROW TOWARDS EACH TO GET THE BALL ROLLING.

_____

_____

LOOK BACK AT THE HABITS YOU ARE WORKING TO BUILD OR BREAK IN YOUR WEEKLY REFLECTION. HOW DID YOU DO? WHERE DID YOU SHOW DISCIPLINE AND WHERE DID YOU DEFAULT?

_____

_____

_____

_____

IF YOU DEFAULTED BACK TO A HABIT YOU ARE TRYING TO BREAK, HOW CAN YOU REINFORCE YOUR WHY AND/OR MOVE FORWARD IN A MORE ALIGNED WAY? IS THERE A SMALLER STEP YOU CAN TAKE FIRST THAT WOULD MAKE THE TRANSITION EASIER OR FEEL LEST RESISTANT?

_____

_____

_____

_____

DID YOU LEARN ANYTHING NEW ABOUT YOURSELF, YOUR GOALS, THE WAY YOU TRACK PROGRESS OR SOMETHING ELSE? IF SO, WRITE IT DOWN BELOW.

_____

_____

_____

_____

USE THE SPACE BELOW FOR ANY ADDITIONAL NOTES:

TAKE A MOMENT TO AFFIRM THE FOLLOWING:
I am exactly where I need to be right now. I fully accept myself as I am, where I am. I am capable, focused, and moving forward with purpose. I celebrate today's wins and welcome tomorrow's opportunities. I release judgment. I am worthy of everything I desire.

Check In Day:

Take a moment to check in, connect with your body, and track your progression through reflection. Skip any sections that don't apply or that don't resonate. Answer each question by reflecting on your experiences, progress, and challenges since your last check-in. Note any changes or anything else that stands out to you.

Gratitude Practice:

List at least 3 things for which you are grateful and why.

_____

_____

_____

_____

Physical Check In:

HOW DO YOU FEEL PHYSICALLY RIGHT NOW?

IN WHAT WAYS CAN YOU SUPPORT OR HONOR YOUR BODY AT THIS TIME?

_____

Emotional Check In:

HOW DO YOU FEEL EMOTIONALLY RIGHT NOW?

What is contributing to how you feel Emotionally?

_____

LIST ANY REOCCURRING EMOTIONS YOU RECALL FEELING.

What might these reoccurring feelings be telling you or what can you learn from them?

_____

WHAT ARE YOU DISAPPOINTED OR DISCONTENT WITH AND WHY?

_____

_____

_____

_____

_____

HOW CAN YOU RESOLVE, HEAL OR CHANGE WHAT YOU FEEL DISAPPOINTED OR DISCONTENT WITH? OR, HOW CAN YOU SUPPORT YOURSELF AT THIS TIME IF A RESOLUTION,CHANGE OR HEALING IS NOT POSSIBLE AT THIS TIME?

_____

_____

_____

_____

_____

WHAT BROUGHT YOU JOY, PEACE, CONTENTMENT AND/OR HAPPINESS?

WHAT DO YOU FEEL PROUD OF OR PROUD OF YOURSELF FOR?

_____

_____

_____

Mental Check In:

HOW DO YOU FEEL MENTALLY RIGHT NOW?

What is contributing to how you feel Mentally?

_____

_____

LIST ANY RECURRING THOUGHTS YOU RECALL HAVING.

_____

_____

_____

WHAT MIGHT THESE RECURRING THOUGHTS BE TELLING YOU? WHAT CAN YOU GLEAN FROM THEM?

_____

_____

_____

LIST ANY LIMITING BELIEFS OR LIMITING THOUGHTS YOU RECALL HAVING.

_____

_____

HOW CAN YOU CHALLENGE OR REFRAME EACH OF THE ABOVE?

_____

_____

_____

Spiritual Check In:

HOW DO YOU FEEL SPIRITUALLY RIGHT NOW?

What is contributing to how you feel spiritually?

_____

_____

PROGRESSION THOUGH REFLECTION

WHAT DRAINED YOUR ENERGY ?

_____

_____

_____

_____

WHAT GAVE YOU ENERGY ?

_____

_____

_____

_____

Did you feel fully grounded and present?   ◯ Yes   ◯ No
If yes, what contributed to this feeling?

If no, how can you foster more presence and ground yourself?

Did you honor your boundaries?   ◯ Yes   ◯ No
If no, how can you better honor your boundaries moving forward?

Did you honor your values and priorities?   ◯ Yes   ◯ No
If yes, how? Was it in the way you expected and if not, how did it differ from your expectations?

If no, what got in the way and how can you better honor your values and priorities moving forward?

HOW DID YOU NUTURE YOURSELF?
(Food, rest, movement, connection, spiritual practice, grounding, creativity, play, fun, other.)

_____

IS THERE ANYTHING YOU NEED RIGHT NOW THAT YOU ARE NOT GIVING YOURSELF?

_____

_____

Check in with your goals & progress:
DID YOU TAKE ANY STEPS TOWARDS ANY OF YOUR GOALS OR DO ANYTHING SMALL THAT ALIGNS WITH THE BIGGER VISION YOU HAVE FOR YOURSELF ?   ◯ Yes ◯ No
If yes, how? If no, what got in the way and what can you do differently tomorrow?

_____

_____

LIST ANY GOALS THAT NEED MORE ATTENTION:

_____

_____

LIST A SMALL STEP YOU CAN TAKE TOMORROW TOWARDS EACH TO GET THE BALL ROLLING.

_____

_____

LOOK BACK AT THE HABITS YOU ARE WORKING TO BUILD OR BREAK IN YOUR WEEKLY REFLECTION. HOW DID YOU DO? WHERE DID YOU SHOW DISCIPLINE AND WHERE DID YOU DEFAULT?

_____

_____

_____

_____

IF YOU DEFAULTED BACK TO A HABIT YOU ARE TRYING TO BREAK, HOW CAN YOU REINFORCE YOUR WHY AND/OR MOVE FORWARD IN A MORE ALIGNED WAY? IS THERE A SMALLER STEP YOU CAN TAKE FIRST THAT WOULD MAKE THE TRANSITION EASIER OR FEEL LEST RESISTANT?

_____

_____

_____

_____

DID YOU LEARN ANYTHING NEW ABOUT YOURSELF, YOUR GOALS, THE WAY YOU TRACK PROGRESS OR SOMETHING ELSE? IF SO, WRITE IT DOWN BELOW.

_____

_____

_____

_____

USE THE SPACE BELOW FOR ANY ADDITIONAL NOTES:

TAKE A MOMENT TO AFFIRM THE FOLLOWING:
I am exactly where I need to be right now. I fully accept myself as I am, where I am. I am capable, focused, and moving forward with purpose. I celebrate today's wins and welcome tomorrow's opportunities. I release judgment. I am worthy of everything I desire.

CHAPTER
Nine: Week Eight

WEEKLY CHECK IN:

LIST ANY SYNCHRONICITIES YOU NOTICE FROM LAST WEEK'S REFLECTION OR IN YOUR LIFE IN GENERAL:

LIST ANY CHANGES OR ADJUSTMENTS YOU NEED TO MAKE & WHY:

GOALS:

WITH THE ABOVE & THE INFORMATION YOU WROTE IN YOUR MONTHLY SECTION IN MIND, MAKE A LIST OF GOALS YOU WOULD LIKE TO ACCOMPLISH & WHY.

It may help to put your goal in this format: I want to accomplish_____ because _____.

125

FOR EACH OF THE GOALS LISTED, WRITE ONE OR MORE STEP(S) YOU CAN TAKE TO BRING YOU CLOSER TO REACHING EACH GOAL.

NOW PICK ONLY 3 TASKS ABOVE TO FOCUS ON THIS WEEK BY MARKING THEM WITH A STAR, HIGHLIGHTING, OR NUMBERING THEM.

Choose the three tasks that feel most aligned with your journey right now—whether that's what you're most intuitively drawn to, most excited about or what feels highest in priority. If priority is important to you this week, try numbering them from 1 to 3, with 1 being the most important. Choosing only three tasks at one time will keep the path forward clear and focused while limiting feelings of overwhelm.

Remember, if you finish these three tasks before the week is over, you can always come back to this page and take the next step. Use the extra space below if you need more room to organize your tasks or want to tackle a second group of tasks after completing the first this week.

MAKE A LIST OF HABITS YOU WOULD LIKE TO BUILD OR BREAK RIGHT NOW. THEN LIST HOW EACH WILL SUPPORT THE VERSION OF YOU THAT YOU DESIRE FOR YOURSELF.

It may help to put your habits in this format: I want to break/build_____habit, because _____.

Check In Day:

DATE: /   /

Take a moment to check in, connect with your body, and track your progression through reflection. Skip any sections that don't apply or that don't resonate. Answer each question by reflecting on your experiences, progress, and challenges since your last check-in. Note any changes or anything else that stands out to you.

Gratitude Practice:

List at least 3 things for which you are grateful and why.

_____

_____

_____

_____

Physical Check In:

HOW DO YOU FEEL PHYSICALLY RIGHT NOW?

IN WHAT WAYS CAN YOU SUPPORT OR HONOR YOUR BODY AT THIS TIME?

_____   _____

_____   _____

Emotional Check In:

HOW DO YOU FEEL EMOTIONALLY RIGHT NOW?

What is contributing to how you feel Emotionally?

_____

_____

LIST ANY REOCCURRING EMOTIONS YOU RECALL FEELING.

What might these reoccurring feelings be telling you or what can you learn from them?

_____

_____

127

PROGRESSION THOUGH REFLECTION

WHAT ARE YOU DISAPPOINTED OR DISCONTENT WITH AND WHY?

_____

_____

_____

_____

_____

HOW CAN YOU RESOLVE, HEAL OR CHANGE WHAT YOU FEEL DISAPPOINTED OR DISCONTENT WITH? OR, HOW CAN YOU SUPPORT YOURSELF AT THIS TIME IF A RESOLUTION,CHANGE OR HEALING IS NOT POSSIBLE AT THIS TIME?

_____

_____

_____

_____

_____

WHAT BROUGHT YOU JOY, PEACE, CONTENTMENT AND/OR HAPPINESS?

WHAT DO YOU FEEL PROUD OF OR PROUD OF YOURSELF FOR?

_____

_____

_____

Mental Check In:

| HOW DO YOU FEEL MENTALLY RIGHT NOW? |

What is contributing to how you feel Mentally?

_____

_____

LIST ANY RECURRING THOUGHTS YOU RECALL HAVING.

_____

_____

_____

WHAT MIGHT THESE RECURRING THOUGHTS BE TELLING YOU? WHAT CAN YOU GLEAN FROM THEM?

_____

_____

_____

LIST ANY LIMITING BELIEFS OR LIMITING THOUGHTS YOU RECALL HAVING.

_____

_____

_____

HOW CAN YOU CHALLENGE OR REFRAME EACH OF THE ABOVE?

_____

_____

_____

Spiritual Check In:

HOW DO YOU FEEL SPIRITUALLY RIGHT NOW?

What is contributing to how you feel spiritually?

_____

_____

PROGRESSION THOUGH REFLECTION

WHAT DRAINED YOUR ENERGY ?

_____

_____

_____

_____

WHAT GAVE YOU ENERGY ?

_____

_____

_____

_____

Did you feel fully grounded and present?   ◯ Yes   ◯ No
If yes, what contributed to this feeling?

If no, how can you foster more presence and ground yourself?

Did you honor your boundaries?   ◯ Yes   ◯ No
If no, how can you better honor your boundaries moving forward?

Did you honor your values and priorities?   ◯ Yes   ◯ No
If yes, how? Was it in the way you expected and if not, how did it differ from your expectations?

If no, what got in the way and how can you better honor your values and priorities moving forward?

HOW DID YOU NUTURE YOURSELF?
(Food, rest, movement, connection, spiritual practice, grounding, creativity, play, fun, other.)

_____

IS THERE ANYTHING YOU NEED RIGHT NOW THAT YOU ARE NOT GIVING YOURSELF?

_____

_____

Check in with your goals & progress:
**DID YOU TAKE ANY STEPS TOWARDS ANY OF YOUR GOALS OR DO ANYTHING SMALL
THAT ALIGNS WITH THE BIGGER VISION YOU HAVE FOR YOURSELF ?**   ◯ Yes ◯ No
If yes, how? If no, what got in the way and what can you do differently tomorrow?

_____

_____

_____

LIST ANY GOALS THAT NEED MORE ATTENTION:

_____

_____

LIST A SMALL STEP YOU CAN TAKE TOMORROW TOWARDS EACH TO GET THE BALL ROLLING.

_____

_____

LOOK BACK AT THE HABITS YOU ARE WORKING TO BUILD OR BREAK IN YOUR WEEKLY REFLECTION. HOW DID YOU DO? WHERE DID YOU SHOW DISCIPLINE AND WHERE DID YOU DEFAULT?

_____

_____

_____

_____

IF YOU DEFAULTED BACK TO A HABIT YOU ARE TRYING TO BREAK, HOW CAN YOU REINFORCE YOUR WHY AND/OR MOVE FORWARD IN A MORE ALIGNED WAY? IS THERE A SMALLER STEP YOU CAN TAKE FIRST THAT WOULD MAKE THE TRANSITION EASIER OR FEEL LEST RESISTANT?

_____

_____

_____

_____

DID YOU LEARN ANYTHING NEW ABOUT YOURSELF, YOUR GOALS, THE WAY YOU TRACK PROGRESS OR SOMETHING ELSE? IF SO, WRITE IT DOWN BELOW.

_____

_____

_____

_____

USE THE SPACE BELOW FOR ANY ADDITIONAL NOTES:

TAKE A MOMENT TO AFFIRM THE FOLLOWING:
I am exactly where I need to be right now. I fully accept myself as I am, where I am. I am capable, focused, and moving forward with purpose. I celebrate today's wins and welcome tomorrow's opportunities. I release judgment. I am worthy of everything I desire.

Check In Day:

DATE: /   /

Take a moment to check in, connect with your body, and track your progression through reflection. Skip any sections that don't apply or that don't resonate. Answer each question by reflecting on your experiences, progress, and challenges since your last check-in. Note any changes or anything else that stands out to you.

Gratitude Practice:

List at least 3 things for which you are grateful and why.

_____

_____

_____

_____

Physical Check In:

HOW DO YOU FEEL PHYSICALLY RIGHT NOW?

IN WHAT WAYS CAN YOU SUPPORT OR HONOR YOUR BODY AT THIS TIME?

_____

_____

_____

_____

Emotional Check In:

HOW DO YOU FEEL EMOTIONALLY RIGHT NOW?

What is contributing to how you feel Emotionally?

_____

_____

LIST ANY REOCCURRING EMOTIONS YOU RECALL FEELING.

What might these reoccurring feelings be telling you or what can you learn from them?

_____

_____

WHAT ARE YOU DISAPPOINTED OR DISCONTENT WITH AND WHY?

_____

_____

_____

_____

_____

HOW CAN YOU RESOLVE, HEAL OR CHANGE WHAT YOU FEEL DISAPPOINTED OR DISCONTENT WITH? OR, HOW CAN YOU SUPPORT YOURSELF AT THIS TIME IF A RESOLUTION,CHANGE OR HEALING IS NOT POSSIBLE AT THIS TIME?

_____

_____

_____

_____

_____

WHAT BROUGHT YOU JOY, PEACE, CONTENTMENT AND/OR HAPPINESS?

WHAT DO YOU FEEL PROUD OF OR PROUD OF YOURSELF FOR?

_____

_____

_____

Mental Check In:

HOW DO YOU FEEL MENTALLY RIGHT NOW?

What is contributing to how you feel Mentally?

_____

_____

LIST ANY RECURRING THOUGHTS YOU RECALL HAVING.

_____

_____

_____

WHAT MIGHT THESE RECURRING THOUGHTS BE TELLING YOU? WHAT CAN YOU GLEAN FROM THEM?

_____

_____

_____

LIST ANY LIMITING BELIEFS OR LIMITING THOUGHTS YOU RECALL HAVING.

_____

_____

HOW CAN YOU CHALLENGE OR REFRAME EACH OF THE ABOVE?

_____

_____

_____

Spiritual Check In:

HOW DO YOU FEEL SPIRITUALLY RIGHT NOW?

What is contributing to how you feel spiritually?

_____

_____

134

WHAT DRAINED YOUR ENERGY ?

_____

_____

_____

_____

WHAT GAVE YOU ENERGY ?

_____

_____

_____

_____

Did you feel fully grounded and present?   ◯ Yes   ◯ No
If yes, what contributed to this feeling?

_____

If no, how can you foster more presence and ground yourself?

_____

Did you honor your boundaries?   ◯ Yes   ◯ No
If no, how can you better honor your boundaries moving forward?

_____

Did you honor your values and priorities?   ◯ Yes   ◯ No
If yes, how? Was it in the way you expected and if not, how did it differ from your expectations?

_____

If no, what got in the way and how can you better honor your values and priorities moving forward?

_____

HOW DID YOU NUTURE YOURSELF?
(Food, rest, movement, connection, spiritual practice, grounding, creativity, play, fun, other.)

_____

IS THERE ANYTHING YOU NEED RIGHT NOW THAT YOU ARE NOT GIVING YOURSELF?

_____

_____

Check in with your goals & progress:

DID YOU TAKE ANY STEPS TOWARDS ANY OF YOUR GOALS OR DO ANYTHING SMALL THAT ALIGNS WITH THE BIGGER VISION YOU HAVE FOR YOURSELF ?   ◯ Yes ◯ No
If yes, how? If no, what got in the way and what can you do differently tomorrow?

_____

_____

LIST ANY GOALS THAT NEED MORE ATTENTION:

_____

_____

135

PROGRESSION THOUGH REFLECTION

LIST A SMALL STEP YOU CAN TAKE TOMORROW TOWARDS EACH TO GET THE BALL ROLLING.

_____

_____

LOOK BACK AT THE HABITS YOU ARE WORKING TO BUILD OR BREAK IN YOUR WEEKLY REFLECTION. HOW DID YOU DO? WHERE DID YOU SHOW DISCIPLINE AND WHERE DID YOU DEFAULT?

_____

_____

_____

_____

IF YOU DEFAULTED BACK TO A HABIT YOU ARE TRYING TO BREAK, HOW CAN YOU REINFORCE YOUR WHY AND/OR MOVE FORWARD IN A MORE ALIGNED WAY? IS THERE A SMALLER STEP YOU CAN TAKE FIRST THAT WOULD MAKE THE TRANSITION EASIER OR FEEL LEST RESISTANT?

_____

_____

_____

_____

DID YOU LEARN ANYTHING NEW ABOUT YOURSELF, YOUR GOALS, THE WAY YOU TRACK PROGRESS OR SOMETHING ELSE? IF SO, WRITE IT DOWN BELOW.

_____

_____

_____

_____

USE THE SPACE BELOW FOR ANY ADDITIONAL NOTES:

TAKE A MOMENT TO AFFIRM THE FOLLOWING:
I am exactly where I need to be right now. I fully accept myself as I am, where I am. I am capable, focused, and moving forward with purpose. I celebrate today's wins and welcome tomorrow's opportunities. I release judgment. I am worthy of everything I desire.

Check In Day:

Take a moment to check in, connect with your body, and track your progression through reflection. Skip any sections that don't apply or that don't resonate. Answer each question by reflecting on your experiences, progress, and challenges since your last check-in. Note any changes or anything else that stands out to you.

Gratitude Practice:

List at least 3 things for which you are grateful and why.

_____

_____

_____

_____

Physical Check In:

| HOW DO YOU FEEL PHYSICALLY RIGHT NOW? | IN WHAT WAYS CAN YOU SUPPORT OR HONOR YOUR BODY AT THIS TIME? |

_____

Emotional Check In:

| HOW DO YOU FEEL EMOTIONALLY RIGHT NOW? | What is contributing to how you feel Emotionally? |

_____

| LIST ANY REOCCURRING EMOTIONS YOU RECALL FEELING. | What might these reoccurring feelings be telling you or what can you learn from them? |

_____

137

WHAT ARE YOU DISAPPOINTED OR DISCONTENT WITH AND WHY?

_____

_____

_____

_____

_____

HOW CAN YOU RESOLVE, HEAL OR CHANGE WHAT YOU FEEL DISAPPOINTED OR DISCONTENT WITH? OR, HOW CAN YOU SUPPORT YOURSELF AT THIS TIME IF A RESOLUTION,CHANGE OR HEALING IS NOT POSSIBLE AT THIS TIME?

_____

_____

_____

_____

_____

WHAT BROUGHT YOU JOY, PEACE, CONTENTMENT AND/OR HAPPINESS?

WHAT DO YOU FEEL PROUD OF OR PROUD OF YOURSELF FOR?

_____

_____

_____

Mental Check In:

HOW DO YOU FEEL MENTALLY RIGHT NOW?

What is contributing to how you feel Mentally?

_____

_____

138

LIST ANY RECURRING THOUGHTS YOU RECALL HAVING.

_____

_____

_____

WHAT MIGHT THESE RECURRING THOUGHTS BE TELLING YOU? WHAT CAN YOU GLEAN FROM THEM?

_____

_____

_____

LIST ANY LIMITING BELIEFS OR LIMITING THOUGHTS YOU RECALL HAVING.

_____

_____

_____

HOW CAN YOU CHALLENGE OR REFRAME EACH OF THE ABOVE?

_____

_____

_____

Spiritual Check In:

HOW DO YOU FEEL SPIRITUALLY RIGHT NOW?

What is contributing to how you feel spiritually?

_____

_____

PROGRESSION THOUGH REFLECTION

WHAT DRAINED YOUR ENERGY ?

_____

_____

_____

_____

WHAT GAVE YOU ENERGY ?

_____

_____

_____

_____

Did you feel fully grounded and present?   ◯ Yes   ◯ No

If yes, what contributed to this feeling?

_____

If no, how can you foster more presence and ground yourself?

_____

Did you honor your boundaries?   ◯ Yes   ◯ No

If no, how can you better honor your boundaries moving forward?

_____

Did you honor your values and priorities?   ◯ Yes   ◯ No

If yes, how? Was it in the way you expected and if not, how did it differ from your expectations?

_____

If no, what got in the way and how can you better honor your values and priorities moving forward?

_____

HOW DID YOU NUTURE YOURSELF?
(Food, rest, movement, connection, spiritual practice, grounding, creativity, play, fun, other.)

_____

IS THERE ANYTHING YOU NEED RIGHT NOW THAT YOU ARE NOT GIVING YOURSELF?

_____

_____

Check in with your goals & progress:
DID YOU TAKE ANY STEPS TOWARDS ANY OF YOUR GOALS OR DO ANYTHING SMALL THAT ALIGNS WITH THE BIGGER VISION YOU HAVE FOR YOURSELF ?   ◯ Yes ◯ No

If yes, how? If no, what got in the way and what can you do differently tomorrow?

_____

_____

LIST ANY GOALS THAT NEED MORE ATTENTION:

_____

_____

LIST A SMALL STEP YOU CAN TAKE TOMORROW TOWARDS EACH TO GET THE BALL ROLLING.

_____

_____

LOOK BACK AT THE HABITS YOU ARE WORKING TO BUILD OR BREAK IN YOUR WEEKLY REFLECTION. HOW DID YOU DO? WHERE DID YOU SHOW DISCIPLINE AND WHERE DID YOU DEFAULT?

_____

_____

_____

_____

IF YOU DEFAULTED BACK TO A HABIT YOU ARE TRYING TO BREAK, HOW CAN YOU REINFORCE YOUR WHY AND/OR MOVE FORWARD IN A MORE ALIGNED WAY? IS THERE A SMALLER STEP YOU CAN TAKE FIRST THAT WOULD MAKE THE TRANSITION EASIER OR FEEL LEST RESISTANT?

_____

_____

_____

_____

DID YOU LEARN ANYTHING NEW ABOUT YOURSELF, YOUR GOALS, THE WAY YOU TRACK PROGRESS OR SOMETHING ELSE? IF SO, WRITE IT DOWN BELOW.

_____

_____

_____

_____

USE THE SPACE BELOW FOR ANY ADDITIONAL NOTES:

TAKE A MOMENT TO AFFIRM THE FOLLOWING:
I am exactly where I need to be right now. I fully accept myself as I am, where I am. I am capable, focused, and moving forward with purpose. I celebrate today's wins and welcome tomorrow's opportunities. I release judgment. I am worthy of everything I desire.

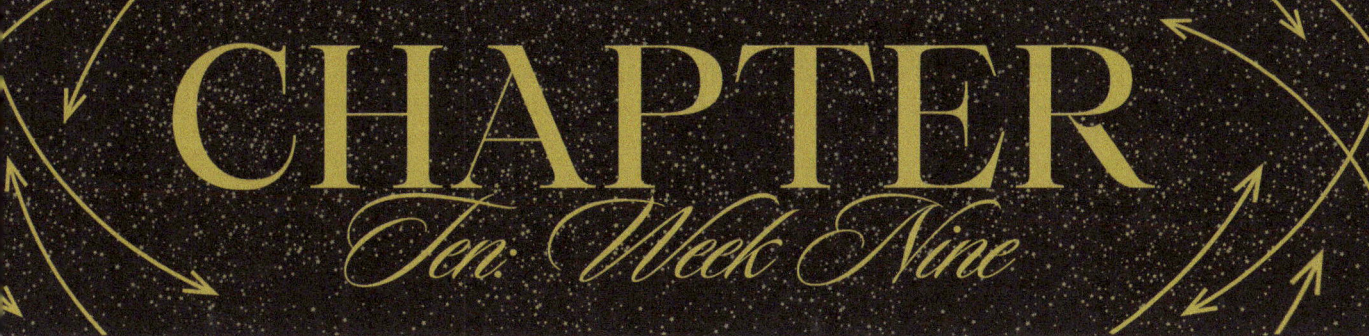
THIRD MONTHLY CHECK IN:

DATE: /   /

Let's get a sense of where you are and where you want to be...

HOW ARE YOU FEELING & WHAT IS CONTRIBUTING TO THESE FEELINGS...

PHYSICALLY:

EMOTIONALLY:

MENTALLY:

SPIRITUALLY:

IN RELATIONSHIPS:

IN CAREER:

SOCIALLY:

FINANCIALLY:

PROGRESSION THOUGH REFLECTION

IF ANYTHING WERE POSSIBLE, AND NOTHING AND NOBODY STOOD IN YOUR WAY, AND YOU COULD HAVE AND BE ANYTHING YOU COULD EVER WANT, WHAT WOULD IT BE? WHAT DO YOU WANT?

If you find this question difficult to answer, think about what you don't want first and then write the opposite.

PHYSICALLY: **EMOTIONALLY:**   **MENTALLY:**   **SPIRITUALLY:**

IN RELATIONSHIPS: **IN CAREER:**   **SOCIALLY:**   **FINANCIALLY:**

AND HOW WOULD YOU WANT TO FEEL...

PHYSICALLY: **EMOTIONALLY:**   **MENTALLY:**   **SPIRITUALLY:**

IN RELATIONSHIPS: **IN CAREER:**   **SOCIALLY:**   **FINANCIALLY:**

143

LIST ANYTHING THAT IS NOT CURRENTLY SERVING YOU OR THE VERSION OF YOU THAT YOU DESIRE TO BE IN ANY OF THE LISTED AREAS.

_____

_____

_____

_____

_____

_____

IN GENERAL, WHAT MAKES YOU FEEL REGULATED, AT PEACE AND/OR JOYFUL...

PHYSICALLY:　　　**EMOTIONALLY:**　　　**MENTALLY:**　　　**SPIRITUALLY:**

IN RELATIONSHIPS:　　　**IN CAREER:**　　　**SOCIALLY:**　　　**FINANCIALLY:**

BASED ON EVERYTHING YOU HAVE WRITTEN SO FAR, SEE IF YOU CAN IDENTIFY THE ROOT ENERGIES OF YOUR NEEDS & DESIRES. WHAT DO YOU ACTUALLY VALUE AND PRIORITIZE OR WHAT DO YOU WANT TO VALUE/PRIORITIZE...

PHYSICALLY:　　　**EMOTIONALLY:**　　　**MENTALLY:**　　　**SPIRITUALLY:**

PROGRESSION THOUGH REFLECTION

IN RELATIONSHIPS: **IN CAREER:**   **SOCIALLY:**   **FINANCIALLY:**

WHAT HABITS SUPPORT OR HINDER YOUR DESIRES, VALUES AND PRIORITIES...

PHYSICALLY: **EMOTIONALLY:**   **MENTALLY:**   **SPIRITUALLY:**

IN RELATIONSHIPS: **IN CAREER:**   **SOCIALLY:**   **FINANCIALLY:**

GOALS:

WITH THE ABOVE INFORMATION IN MIND, MAKE A LIST OF GOALS YOU WOULD LIKE TO ACCOMPLISH & WHY.

It may help to put your goal in this format: I want to accomplish_____ because _____.

FOR EACH OF THE GOALS YOU LISTED, WRITE ONE OR MORE STEP(S) YOU CAN TAKE TO BRING YOU CLOSER TO EACH GOAL.

NOW PICK ONLY 3 TASKS ABOVE TO FOCUS ON THIS WEEK BY MARKING THEM WITH A STAR, HIGHLIGHTING, OR NUMBERING THEM.

Choose the three tasks that feel most aligned with your journey right now—whether that's what you're most intuitively drawn to, most excited about or what feels highest in priority. If priority is important to you this week, try numbering them from 1 to 3, with 1 being the most important. Choosing only three tasks at one time will keep the path forward clear and focused while limiting feelings of overwhelm.

Remember, if you finish these three tasks before the week is over, you can always come back to this page and take the next step. Use the extra space below if you need more room to organize your tasks or want to tackle a second group of tasks after completing the first this week.

MAKE A LIST OF ANY HABITS YOU WOULD LIKE TO BUILD OR BREAK RIGHT NOW. THEN LIST HOW EACH WILL SUPPORT THE VERSION OF YOU THAT YOU DESIRE FOR YOURSELF. (It may help to put your habits in this format: I want to break/build_____ habit, because _____.)

Check In Day:

DATE: /   /

Take a moment to check in, connect with your body, and track your progression through reflection. Skip any sections that don't apply or that don't resonate. Answer each question by reflecting on your experiences, progress, and challenges since your last check-in. Note any changes or anything else that stands out to you.

Gratitude Practice:

List at least 3 things for which you are grateful and why.

_____

_____

_____

_____

Physical Check In:

HOW DO YOU FEEL PHYSICALLY RIGHT NOW?

IN WHAT WAYS CAN YOU SUPPORT OR HONOR YOUR BODY AT THIS TIME?

_____   _____

_____   _____

Emotional Check In:

HOW DO YOU FEEL EMOTIONALLY RIGHT NOW?

What is contributing to how you feel Emotionally?

_____

_____

LIST ANY REOCCURRING EMOTIONS YOU RECALL FEELING.

What might these reoccurring feelings be telling you or what can you learn from them?

_____

_____

WHAT ARE YOU DISAPPOINTED OR DISCONTENT WITH AND WHY?

_____

_____

_____

_____

_____

HOW CAN YOU RESOLVE, HEAL OR CHANGE WHAT YOU FEEL DISAPPOINTED OR DISCONTENT WITH? OR, HOW CAN YOU SUPPORT YOURSELF AT THIS TIME IF A RESOLUTION,CHANGE OR HEALING IS NOT POSSIBLE AT THIS TIME?

_____

_____

_____

_____

_____

WHAT BROUGHT YOU JOY, PEACE, CONTENTMENT AND/OR HAPPINESS?

WHAT DO YOU FEEL PROUD OF OR PROUD OF YOURSELF FOR?

_____

_____

_____

Mental Check In:

HOW DO YOU FEEL
MENTALLY RIGHT NOW?

What is contributing to how you feel Mentally?

_____

_____

LIST ANY RECURRING THOUGHTS YOU RECALL HAVING.

_____

_____

_____

WHAT MIGHT THESE RECURRING THOUGHTS BE TELLING YOU? WHAT CAN YOU GLEAN FROM THEM?

_____

_____

_____

LIST ANY LIMITING BELIEFS OR LIMITING THOUGHTS YOU RECALL HAVING.

_____

_____

_____

HOW CAN YOU CHALLENGE OR REFRAME EACH OF THE ABOVE?

_____

_____

_____

Spiritual Check In:

HOW DO YOU FEEL SPIRITUALLY RIGHT NOW?

What is contributing to how you feel spiritually?

_____

_____

WHAT DRAINED YOUR ENERGY ?

_____

_____

_____

_____

Did you feel fully grounded and present?

If yes, what contributed to this feeling?

_____

If no, how can you foster more presence and ground yourself?

_____

Did you honor your boundaries?

If no, how can you better honor your boundaries moving forward?

_____

Did you honor your values and priorities?

If yes, how? Was it in the way you expected and if not, how did it differ from your expectations?

_____

If no, what got in the way and how can you better honor your values and priorities moving forward?

_____

WHAT GAVE YOU ENERGY ?

_____

_____

_____

_____

◯ Yes   ◯ No

◯ Yes   ◯ No

◯ Yes   ◯ No

HOW DID YOU NUTURE YOURSELF?
(Food, rest, movement, connection, spiritual practice, grounding, creativity, play, fun, other.)

_____

IS THERE ANYTHING YOU NEED RIGHT NOW THAT YOU ARE NOT GIVING YOURSELF?

_____

_____

Check in with your goals & progress:
DID YOU TAKE ANY STEPS TOWARDS ANY OF YOUR GOALS OR DO ANYTHING SMALL THAT ALIGNS WITH THE BIGGER VISION YOU HAVE FOR YOURSELF ?   ◯ Yes   ◯ No

If yes, how? If no, what got in the way and what can you do differently tomorrow?

_____

_____

LIST ANY GOALS THAT NEED MORE ATTENTION:

_____

_____

PROGRESSION THOUGH REFLECTION

LIST A SMALL STEP YOU CAN TAKE TOMORROW TOWARDS EACH TO GET THE BALL ROLLING.

_____

_____

LOOK BACK AT THE HABITS YOU ARE WORKING TO BUILD OR BREAK IN YOUR MONTHLY REFLECTION. HOW DID YOU DO? WHERE DID YOU SHOW DISCIPLINE AND WHERE DID YOU DEFAULT?

_____

_____

_____

IF YOU DEFAULTED BACK TO A HABIT YOU ARE TRYING TO BREAK, HOW CAN YOU REINFORCE YOUR WHY AND/OR MOVE FORWARD IN A MORE ALIGNED WAY? IS THERE A SMALLER STEP YOU CAN TAKE FIRST THAT WOULD MAKE THE TRANSITION EASIER OR FEEL LEST RESISTANT?

_____

_____

_____

DID YOU LEARN ANYTHING NEW ABOUT YOURSELF, YOUR GOALS, THE WAY YOU TRACK PROGRESS OR SOMETHING ELSE? IF SO, WRITE IT DOWN BELOW.

_____

_____

_____

USE THE SPACE BELOW FOR ANY ADDITIONAL NOTES:

TAKE A MOMENT TO AFFIRM THE FOLLOWING:
I am exactly where I need to be right now. I fully accept myself as I am, where I am. I am capable, focused, and moving forward with purpose. I celebrate today's wins and welcome tomorrow's opportunities. I release judgment. I am worthy of everything I desire.

Check In Day:

Take a moment to check in, connect with your body, and track your progression through reflection. Skip any sections that don't apply or that don't resonate. Answer each question by reflecting on your experiences, progress, and challenges since your last check-in. Note any changes or anything else that stands out to you.

Gratitude Practice:

List at least 3 things for which you are grateful and why.

_____

_____

_____

_____

Physical Check In:

| HOW DO YOU FEEL PHYSICALLY RIGHT NOW? | IN WHAT WAYS CAN YOU SUPPORT OR HONOR YOUR BODY AT THIS TIME? |

_____   _____

_____   _____

Emotional Check In:

| HOW DO YOU FEEL EMOTIONALLY RIGHT NOW? |

What is contributing to how you feel Emotionally?

_____   _____

_____   _____

| LIST ANY REOCCURRING EMOTIONS YOU RECALL FEELING. |

What might these reoccurring feelings be telling you or what can you learn from them?

_____

_____

PROGRESSION THOUGH REFLECTION

WHAT ARE YOU DISAPPOINTED OR DISCONTENT WITH AND WHY?

_____

_____

_____

_____

_____

HOW CAN YOU RESOLVE, HEAL OR CHANGE WHAT YOU FEEL DISAPPOINTED OR DISCONTENT WITH? OR, HOW CAN YOU SUPPORT YOURSELF AT THIS TIME IF A RESOLUTION,CHANGE OR HEALING IS NOT POSSIBLE AT THIS TIME?

_____

_____

_____

_____

_____

WHAT BROUGHT YOU JOY, PEACE, CONTENTMENT AND/OR HAPPINESS?

WHAT DO YOU FEEL PROUD OF OR PROUD OF YOURSELF FOR?

_____

_____

_____

Mental Check In:

HOW DO YOU FEEL MENTALLY RIGHT NOW?

What is contributing to how you feel Mentally?

_____

_____

LIST ANY RECURRING THOUGHTS YOU RECALL HAVING.

_____

_____

_____

WHAT MIGHT THESE RECURRING THOUGHTS BE TELLING YOU? WHAT CAN YOU GLEAN FROM THEM?

_____

_____

_____

LIST ANY LIMITING BELIEFS OR LIMITING THOUGHTS YOU RECALL HAVING.

_____

_____

_____

HOW CAN YOU CHALLENGE OR REFRAME EACH OF THE ABOVE?

_____

_____

_____

Spiritual Check In:

HOW DO YOU FEEL SPIRITUALLY RIGHT NOW?

What is contributing to how you feel spiritually?

_____

_____

WHAT DRAINED YOUR ENERGY ?

_____

_____

_____

_____

WHAT GAVE YOU ENERGY ?

_____

_____

_____

_____

Did you feel fully grounded and present?   ◯ Yes   ◯ No
If yes, what contributed to this feeling?

_____

If no, how can you foster more presence and ground yourself?

_____

Did you honor your boundaries?   ◯ Yes   ◯ No
If no, how can you better honor your boundaries moving forward?

_____

Did you honor your values and priorities?   ◯ Yes   ◯ No
If yes, how? Was it in the way you expected and if not, how did it differ from your expectations?

_____

If no, what got in the way and how can you better honor your values and priorities moving forward?

_____

HOW DID YOU NUTURE YOURSELF?
(Food, rest, movement, connection, spiritual practice, grounding, creativity, play, fun, other.)

_____

IS THERE ANYTHING YOU NEED RIGHT NOW THAT YOU ARE NOT GIVING YOURSELF?

_____

_____

Check in with your goals & progress:

DID YOU TAKE ANY STEPS TOWARDS ANY OF YOUR GOALS OR DO ANYTHING SMALL THAT ALIGNS WITH THE BIGGER VISION YOU HAVE FOR YOURSELF ?   ◯ Yes   ◯ No
If yes, how? If no, what got in the way and what can you do differently tomorrow?

_____

_____

_____

LIST ANY GOALS THAT NEED MORE ATTENTION:

_____

_____

155

LIST A SMALL STEP YOU CAN TAKE TOMORROW TOWARDS EACH TO GET THE BALL ROLLING.

_____

_____

LOOK BACK AT THE HABITS YOU ARE WORKING TO BUILD OR BREAK IN YOUR MONTHLY REFLECTION. HOW DID YOU DO? WHERE DID YOU SHOW DISCIPLINE AND WHERE DID YOU DEFAULT?

_____

_____

_____

_____

IF YOU DEFAULTED BACK TO A HABIT YOU ARE TRYING TO BREAK, HOW CAN YOU REINFORCE YOUR WHY AND/OR MOVE FORWARD IN A MORE ALIGNED WAY? IS THERE A SMALLER STEP YOU CAN TAKE FIRST THAT WOULD MAKE THE TRANSITION EASIER OR FEEL LEST RESISTANT?

_____

_____

_____

_____

DID YOU LEARN ANYTHING NEW ABOUT YOURSELF, YOUR GOALS, THE WAY YOU TRACK PROGRESS OR SOMETHING ELSE? IF SO, WRITE IT DOWN BELOW.

_____

_____

_____

_____

USE THE SPACE BELOW FOR ANY ADDITIONAL NOTES:

TAKE A MOMENT TO AFFIRM THE FOLLOWING:
I am exactly where I need to be right now. I fully accept myself as I am, where I am. I am capable, focused, and moving forward with purpose. I celebrate today's wins and welcome tomorrow's opportunities. I release judgment. I am worthy of everything I desire.

Check In Day:

Take a moment to check in, connect with your body, and track your progression through reflection. Skip any sections that don't apply or that don't resonate. Answer each question by reflecting on your experiences, progress, and challenges since your last check-in. Note any changes or anything else that stands out to you.

Gratitude Practice:
List at least 3 things for which you are grateful and why.

_____

_____

_____

_____

Physical Check In:

HOW DO YOU FEEL PHYSICALLY RIGHT NOW?

IN WHAT WAYS CAN YOU SUPPORT OR HONOR YOUR BODY AT THIS TIME?

_____   _____

_____   _____

Emotional Check In:

HOW DO YOU FEEL EMOTIONALLY RIGHT NOW?

What is contributing to how you feel Emotionally?

_____

_____

LIST ANY REOCCURRING EMOTIONS YOU RECALL FEELING.

What might these reoccurring feelings be telling you or what can you learn from them?

_____

_____

WHAT ARE YOU DISAPPOINTED OR DISCONTENT WITH AND WHY?

_____

_____

_____

_____

_____

HOW CAN YOU RESOLVE, HEAL OR CHANGE WHAT YOU FEEL DISAPPOINTED OR DISCONTENT WITH? OR, HOW CAN YOU SUPPORT YOURSELF AT THIS TIME IF A RESOLUTION,CHANGE OR HEALING IS NOT POSSIBLE AT THIS TIME?

_____

_____

_____

_____

_____

WHAT BROUGHT YOU JOY, PEACE, CONTENTMENT AND/OR HAPPINESS?

WHAT DO YOU FEEL PROUD OF OR PROUD OF YOURSELF FOR?

_____

_____

_____

Mental Check In:

HOW DO YOU FEEL MENTALLY RIGHT NOW?

What is contributing to how you feel Mentally?

_____

_____

LIST ANY RECURRING THOUGHTS YOU RECALL HAVING.

_____

_____

_____

WHAT MIGHT THESE RECURRING THOUGHTS BE TELLING YOU? WHAT CAN YOU GLEAN FROM THEM?

_____

_____

_____

LIST ANY LIMITING BELIEFS OR LIMITING THOUGHTS YOU RECALL HAVING.

_____

_____

_____

HOW CAN YOU CHALLENGE OR REFRAME EACH OF THE ABOVE?

_____

_____

_____

Spiritual Check In:

HOW DO YOU FEEL SPIRITUALLY RIGHT NOW?

What is contributing to how you feel spiritually?

_____

_____

WHAT DRAINED YOUR ENERGY ?	WHAT GAVE YOU ENERGY ?
_____	_____
_____	_____
_____	_____
_____	_____

Did you feel fully grounded and present?   ◯ Yes   ◯ No

If yes, what contributed to this feeling?

_____

If no, how can you foster more presence and ground yourself?

_____

Did you honor your boundaries?   ◯ Yes   ◯ No

If no, how can you better honor your boundaries moving forward?

_____

Did you honor your values and priorities?   ◯ Yes   ◯ No

If yes, how? Was it in the way you expected and if not, how did it differ from your expectations?

_____

If no, what got in the way and how can you better honor your values and priorities moving forward?

_____

HOW DID YOU NUTURE YOURSELF?
(Food, rest, movement, connection, spiritual practice, grounding, creativity, play, fun, other.)

_____

IS THERE ANYTHING YOU NEED RIGHT NOW THAT YOU ARE NOT GIVING YOURSELF?

_____

_____

Check in with your goals & progress:
DID YOU TAKE ANY STEPS TOWARDS ANY OF YOUR GOALS OR DO ANYTHING SMALL THAT ALIGNS WITH THE BIGGER VISION YOU HAVE FOR YOURSELF ?   ◯ Yes   ◯ No

If yes, how? If no, what got in the way and what can you do differently tomorrow?

_____

_____

LIST ANY GOALS THAT NEED MORE ATTENTION:

_____

_____

PROGRESSION THOUGH REFLECTION

LIST A SMALL STEP YOU CAN TAKE TOMORROW TOWARDS EACH TO GET THE BALL ROLLING.

_____

_____

LOOK BACK AT THE HABITS YOU ARE WORKING TO BUILD OR BREAK IN YOUR MONTHLY REFLECTION. HOW DID YOU DO? WHERE DID YOU SHOW DISCIPLINE AND WHERE DID YOU DEFAULT?

_____

_____

_____

_____

IF YOU DEFAULTED BACK TO A HABIT YOU ARE TRYING TO BREAK, HOW CAN YOU REINFORCE YOUR WHY AND/OR MOVE FORWARD IN A MORE ALIGNED WAY? IS THERE A SMALLER STEP YOU CAN TAKE FIRST THAT WOULD MAKE THE TRANSITION EASIER OR FEEL LEST RESISTANT?

_____

_____

_____

_____

DID YOU LEARN ANYTHING NEW ABOUT YOURSELF, YOUR GOALS, THE WAY YOU TRACK PROGRESS OR SOMETHING ELSE? IF SO, WRITE IT DOWN BELOW.

_____

_____

_____

_____

USE THE SPACE BELOW FOR ANY ADDITIONAL NOTES:

TAKE A MOMENT TO AFFIRM THE FOLLOWING:
I am exactly where I need to be right now. I fully accept myself as I am, where I am. I am capable, focused, and moving forward with purpose. I celebrate today's wins and welcome tomorrow's opportunities. I release judgment. I am worthy of everything I desire.

CHAPTER
Eleven: Week Ten

WEEKLY CHECK IN:

LIST ANY SYNCHRONICITIES YOU NOTICE FROM LAST WEEK'S REFLECTION OR IN YOUR LIFE IN GENERAL:

LIST ANY CHANGES OR ADJUSTMENTS YOU NEED TO MAKE & WHY:

GOALS:

WITH THE ABOVE & THE INFORMATION YOU WROTE IN YOUR MONTHLY SECTION IN MIND, MAKE A LIST OF GOALS YOU WOULD LIKE TO ACCOMPLISH & WHY.

It may help to put your goal in this format: I want to accomplish_____ because _____.

FOR EACH OF THE GOALS LISTED, WRITE ONE OR MORE STEP(S) YOU CAN TAKE TO BRING YOU CLOSER TO REACHING EACH GOAL.

NOW PICK ONLY 3 TASKS ABOVE TO FOCUS ON THIS WEEK BY MARKING THEM WITH A STAR, HIGHLIGHTING, OR NUMBERING THEM.

Choose the three tasks that feel most aligned with your journey right now—whether that's what you're most intuitively drawn to, most excited about or what feels highest in priority. If priority is important to you this week, try numbering them from 1 to 3, with 1 being the most important. Choosing only three tasks at one time will keep the path forward clear and focused while limiting feelings of overwhelm.

Remember, if you finish these three tasks before the week is over, you can always come back to this page and take the next step. Use the extra space below if you need more room to organize your tasks or want to tackle a second group of tasks after completing the first this week.

MAKE A LIST OF HABITS YOU WOULD LIKE TO BUILD OR BREAK RIGHT NOW. THEN LIST HOW EACH WILL SUPPORT THE VERSION OF YOU THAT YOU DESIRE FOR YOURSELF.

It may help to put your habits in this format: I want to break/build_____habit, because _____.

Check In Day:

DATE: /   /

Take a moment to check in, connect with your body, and track your progression through reflection. Skip any sections that don't apply or that don't resonate. Answer each question by reflecting on your experiences, progress, and challenges since your last check-in. Note any changes or anything else that stands out to you.

Gratitude Practice:

List at least 3 things for which you are grateful and why.

_____

_____

_____

_____

Physical Check In:

HOW DO YOU FEEL PHYSICALLY RIGHT NOW?

IN WHAT WAYS CAN YOU SUPPORT OR HONOR YOUR BODY AT THIS TIME?

_____

_____

_____

_____

Emotional Check In:

HOW DO YOU FEEL EMOTIONALLY RIGHT NOW?

What is contributing to how you feel Emotionally?

_____

_____

LIST ANY REOCCURRING EMOTIONS YOU RECALL FEELING.

What might these reoccurring feelings be telling you or what can you learn from them?

_____

_____

WHAT ARE YOU DISAPPOINTED OR DISCONTENT WITH AND WHY?

_____

_____

_____

_____

_____

HOW CAN YOU RESOLVE, HEAL OR CHANGE WHAT YOU FEEL DISAPPOINTED OR DISCONTENT WITH? OR, HOW CAN YOU SUPPORT YOURSELF AT THIS TIME IF A RESOLUTION,CHANGE OR HEALING IS NOT POSSIBLE AT THIS TIME?

_____

_____

_____

_____

_____

WHAT BROUGHT YOU JOY, PEACE, CONTENTMENT AND/OR HAPPINESS?

WHAT DO YOU FEEL PROUD OF OR PROUD OF YOURSELF FOR?

_____

_____

_____

Mental Check In:

| HOW DO YOU FEEL MENTALLY RIGHT NOW? |

What is contributing to how you feel Mentally?

_____

_____

165

LIST ANY RECURRING THOUGHTS YOU RECALL HAVING.

_____

_____

_____

WHAT MIGHT THESE RECURRING THOUGHTS BE TELLING YOU? WHAT CAN YOU GLEAN FROM THEM?

_____

_____

_____

LIST ANY LIMITING BELIEFS OR LIMITING THOUGHTS YOU RECALL HAVING.

_____

_____

HOW CAN YOU CHALLENGE OR REFRAME EACH OF THE ABOVE?

_____

_____

_____

Spiritual Check In:

HOW DO YOU FEEL SPIRITUALLY RIGHT NOW?

What is contributing to how you feel spiritually?

_____

_____

PROGRESSION THOUGH REFLECTION

WHAT DRAINED YOUR ENERGY ?

_____

_____

_____

_____

WHAT GAVE YOU ENERGY ?

_____

_____

_____

_____

Did you feel fully grounded and present?   ◯ Yes   ◯ No

If yes, what contributed to this feeling?

_____

If no, how can you foster more presence and ground yourself?

_____

Did you honor your boundaries?   ◯ Yes   ◯ No

If no, how can you better honor your boundaries moving forward?

_____

Did you honor your values and priorities?   ◯ Yes   ◯ No

If yes, how? Was it in the way you expected and if not, how did it differ from your expectations?

_____

If no, what got in the way and how can you better honor your values and priorities moving forward?

_____

HOW DID YOU NUTURE YOURSELF?
(Food, rest, movement, connection, spiritual practice, grounding, creativity, play, fun, other.)

_____

IS THERE ANYTHING YOU NEED RIGHT NOW THAT YOU ARE NOT GIVING YOURSELF?

_____

_____

Check in with your goals & progress:

DID YOU TAKE ANY STEPS TOWARDS ANY OF YOUR GOALS OR DO ANYTHING SMALL THAT ALIGNS WITH THE BIGGER VISION YOU HAVE FOR YOURSELF ? ◯ Yes ◯ No

If yes, how? If no, what got in the way and what can you do differently tomorrow?

_____

_____

_____

LIST ANY GOALS THAT NEED MORE ATTENTION:

_____

_____

LIST A SMALL STEP YOU CAN TAKE TOMORROW TOWARDS EACH TO GET THE BALL ROLLING.

_____

_____

LOOK BACK AT THE HABITS YOU ARE WORKING TO BUILD OR BREAK IN YOUR WEEKLY REFLECTION. HOW DID YOU DO? WHERE DID YOU SHOW DISCIPLINE AND WHERE DID YOU DEFAULT?

_____

_____

_____

_____

IF YOU DEFAULTED BACK TO A HABIT YOU ARE TRYING TO BREAK, HOW CAN YOU REINFORCE YOUR WHY AND/OR MOVE FORWARD IN A MORE ALIGNED WAY? IS THERE A SMALLER STEP YOU CAN TAKE FIRST THAT WOULD MAKE THE TRANSITION EASIER OR FEEL LEST RESISTANT?

_____

_____

_____

_____

DID YOU LEARN ANYTHING NEW ABOUT YOURSELF, YOUR GOALS, THE WAY YOU TRACK PROGRESS OR SOMETHING ELSE? IF SO, WRITE IT DOWN BELOW.

_____

_____

_____

_____

USE THE SPACE BELOW FOR ANY ADDITIONAL NOTES:

TAKE A MOMENT TO AFFIRM THE FOLLOWING:
I am exactly where I need to be right now. I fully accept myself as I am, where I am. I am capable, focused, and moving forward with purpose. I celebrate today's wins and welcome tomorrow's opportunities. I release judgment. I am worthy of everything I desire.

Check In Day:

Take a moment to check in, connect with your body, and track your progression through reflection. Skip any sections that don't apply or that don't resonate. Answer each question by reflecting on your experiences, progress, and challenges since your last check-in. Note any changes or anything else that stands out to you.

Gratitude Practice:

List at least 3 things for which you are grateful and why.

_____

_____

_____

_____

Physical Check In:

| HOW DO YOU FEEL PHYSICALLY RIGHT NOW? | IN WHAT WAYS CAN YOU SUPPORT OR HONOR YOUR BODY AT THIS TIME? |

_____   _____

_____   _____

Emotional Check In:

| HOW DO YOU FEEL EMOTIONALLY RIGHT NOW? | **What is contributing to how you feel Emotionally?** |

_____

_____

| LIST ANY REOCCURRING EMOTIONS YOU RECALL FEELING. | **What might these reoccurring feelings be telling you or what can you learn from them?** |

_____

_____

WHAT ARE YOU DISAPPOINTED OR DISCONTENT WITH AND WHY?

_____

_____

_____

_____

_____

HOW CAN YOU RESOLVE, HEAL OR CHANGE WHAT YOU FEEL DISAPPOINTED OR DISCONTENT WITH? OR, HOW CAN YOU SUPPORT YOURSELF AT THIS TIME IF A RESOLUTION,CHANGE OR HEALING IS NOT POSSIBLE AT THIS TIME?

_____

_____

_____

_____

_____

WHAT BROUGHT YOU JOY, PEACE, CONTENTMENT AND/OR HAPPINESS?

WHAT DO YOU FEEL PROUD OF OR PROUD OF YOURSELF FOR?

_____

_____

_____

Mental Check In:

HOW DO YOU FEEL MENTALLY RIGHT NOW?

What is contributing to how you feel Mentally?

_____

_____

LIST ANY RECURRING THOUGHTS YOU RECALL HAVING.

_____

_____

_____

WHAT MIGHT THESE RECURRING THOUGHTS BE TELLING YOU? WHAT CAN YOU GLEAN FROM THEM?

_____

_____

_____

LIST ANY LIMITING BELIEFS OR LIMITING THOUGHTS YOU RECALL HAVING.

_____

_____

_____

HOW CAN YOU CHALLENGE OR REFRAME EACH OF THE ABOVE?

_____

_____

_____

Spiritual Check In:

HOW DO YOU FEEL SPIRITUALLY RIGHT NOW?

What is contributing to how you feel spiritually?

_____

_____

WHAT DRAINED YOUR ENERGY ?   **WHAT GAVE YOU ENERGY ?**

_____   _____

_____   _____

_____   _____

_____

Did you feel fully grounded and present?   ◯ Yes   ◯ No

If yes, what contributed to this feeling?

_____

If no, how can you foster more presence and ground yourself?

_____

Did you honor your boundaries?   ◯ Yes   ◯ No

If no, how can you better honor your boundaries moving forward?

_____

Did you honor your values and priorities?   ◯ Yes   ◯ No

If yes, how? Was it in the way you expected and if not, how did it differ from your expectations?

_____

If no, what got in the way and how can you better honor your values and priorities moving forward?

_____

HOW DID YOU NUTURE YOURSELF?
(Food, rest, movement, connection, spiritual practice, grounding, creativity, play, fun, other.)

IS THERE ANYTHING YOU NEED RIGHT NOW THAT YOU ARE NOT GIVING YOURSELF?

_____

_____

Check in with your goals & progress:
DID YOU TAKE ANY STEPS TOWARDS ANY OF YOUR GOALS OR DO ANYTHING SMALL THAT ALIGNS WITH THE BIGGER VISION YOU HAVE FOR YOURSELF ?   ◯ Yes   ◯ No

If yes, how? If no, what got in the way and what can you do differently tomorrow?

_____

_____

LIST ANY GOALS THAT NEED MORE ATTENTION:

_____

_____

LIST A SMALL STEP YOU CAN TAKE TOMORROW TOWARDS EACH TO GET THE BALL ROLLING.

_____

_____

LOOK BACK AT THE HABITS YOU ARE WORKING TO BUILD OR BREAK IN YOUR WEEKLY REFLECTION. HOW DID YOU DO? WHERE DID YOU SHOW DISCIPLINE AND WHERE DID YOU DEFAULT?

_____

_____

_____

_____

IF YOU DEFAULTED BACK TO A HABIT YOU ARE TRYING TO BREAK, HOW CAN YOU REINFORCE YOUR WHY AND/OR MOVE FORWARD IN A MORE ALIGNED WAY? IS THERE A SMALLER STEP YOU CAN TAKE FIRST THAT WOULD MAKE THE TRANSITION EASIER OR FEEL LEST RESISTANT?

_____

_____

_____

_____

DID YOU LEARN ANYTHING NEW ABOUT YOURSELF, YOUR GOALS, THE WAY YOU TRACK PROGRESS OR SOMETHING ELSE? IF SO, WRITE IT DOWN BELOW.

_____

_____

_____

_____

USE THE SPACE BELOW FOR ANY ADDITIONAL NOTES:

TAKE A MOMENT TO AFFIRM THE FOLLOWING:
I am exactly where I need to be right now. I fully accept myself as I am, where I am. I am capable, focused, and moving forward with purpose. I celebrate today's wins and welcome tomorrow's opportunities. I release judgment. I am worthy of everything I desire.

Check In Day:

Take a moment to check in, connect with your body, and track your progression through reflection. Skip any sections that don't apply or that don't resonate. Answer each question by reflecting on your experiences, progress, and challenges since your last check-in. Note any changes or anything else that stands out to you.

Gratitude Practice:

List at least 3 things for which you are grateful and why.

_____

_____

_____

_____

Physical Check In:

HOW DO YOU FEEL PHYSICALLY RIGHT NOW?

IN WHAT WAYS CAN YOU SUPPORT OR HONOR YOUR BODY AT THIS TIME?

_____   _____

_____   _____

Emotional Check In:

HOW DO YOU FEEL EMOTIONALLY RIGHT NOW?

What is contributing to how you feel Emotionally?

_____

_____

LIST ANY REOCCURRING EMOTIONS YOU RECALL FEELING.

What might these reoccurring feelings be telling you or what can you learn from them?

_____

_____

WHAT ARE YOU DISAPPOINTED OR DISCONTENT WITH AND WHY?

_____

_____

_____

_____

_____

HOW CAN YOU RESOLVE, HEAL OR CHANGE WHAT YOU FEEL DISAPPOINTED OR DISCONTENT WITH? OR, HOW CAN YOU SUPPORT YOURSELF AT THIS TIME IF A RESOLUTION,CHANGE OR HEALING IS NOT POSSIBLE AT THIS TIME?

_____

_____

_____

_____

_____

WHAT BROUGHT YOU JOY, PEACE, CONTENTMENT AND/OR HAPPINESS?

WHAT DO YOU FEEL PROUD OF OR PROUD OF YOURSELF FOR?

_____

_____

_____

Mental Check In:

HOW DO YOU FEEL MENTALLY RIGHT NOW?

What is contributing to how you feel Mentally?

_____

_____

LIST ANY RECURRING THOUGHTS YOU RECALL HAVING.

_____

_____

_____

WHAT MIGHT THESE RECURRING THOUGHTS BE TELLING YOU? WHAT CAN YOU GLEAN FROM THEM?

_____

_____

_____

LIST ANY LIMITING BELIEFS OR LIMITING THOUGHTS YOU RECALL HAVING.

_____

_____

_____

HOW CAN YOU CHALLENGE OR REFRAME EACH OF THE ABOVE?

_____

_____

_____

Spiritual Check In:

HOW DO YOU FEEL SPIRITUALLY RIGHT NOW?

What is contributing to how you feel spiritually?

_____

_____

PROGRESSION THOUGH REFLECTION

WHAT DRAINED YOUR ENERGY ?

_____
_____
_____
_____

WHAT GAVE YOU ENERGY ?

_____
_____
_____
_____

Did you feel fully grounded and present?   ◯ Yes   ◯ No
If yes, what contributed to this feeling?

If no, how can you foster more presence and ground yourself?

Did you honor your boundaries?   ◯ Yes   ◯ No
If no, how can you better honor your boundaries moving forward?

Did you honor your values and priorities?   ◯ Yes   ◯ No
If yes, how? Was it in the way you expected and if not, how did it differ from your expectations?

If no, what got in the way and how can you better honor your values and priorities moving forward?

HOW DID YOU NUTURE YOURSELF?
(Food, rest, movement, connection, spiritual practice, grounding, creativity, play, fun, other.)

IS THERE ANYTHING YOU NEED RIGHT NOW THAT YOU ARE NOT GIVING YOURSELF?

Check in with your goals & progress:
**DID YOU TAKE ANY STEPS TOWARDS ANY OF YOUR GOALS OR DO ANYTHING SMALL
THAT ALIGNS WITH THE BIGGER VISION YOU HAVE FOR YOURSELF ?**   ◯ Yes   ◯ No
If yes, how? If no, what got in the way and what can you do differently tomorrow?

LIST ANY GOALS THAT NEED MORE ATTENTION:

LIST A SMALL STEP YOU CAN TAKE TOMORROW TOWARDS EACH TO GET THE BALL ROLLING.

_____

_____

LOOK BACK AT THE HABITS YOU ARE WORKING TO BUILD OR BREAK IN YOUR WEEKLY REFLECTION. HOW DID YOU DO? WHERE DID YOU SHOW DISCIPLINE AND WHERE DID YOU DEFAULT?

_____

_____

_____

_____

IF YOU DEFAULTED BACK TO A HABIT YOU ARE TRYING TO BREAK, HOW CAN YOU REINFORCE YOUR WHY AND/OR MOVE FORWARD IN A MORE ALIGNED WAY? IS THERE A SMALLER STEP YOU CAN TAKE FIRST THAT WOULD MAKE THE TRANSITION EASIER OR FEEL LEST RESISTANT?

_____

_____

_____

_____

DID YOU LEARN ANYTHING NEW ABOUT YOURSELF, YOUR GOALS, THE WAY YOU TRACK PROGRESS OR SOMETHING ELSE? IF SO, WRITE IT DOWN BELOW.

_____

_____

_____

_____

USE THE SPACE BELOW FOR ANY ADDITIONAL NOTES:

TAKE A MOMENT TO AFFIRM THE FOLLOWING:
I am exactly where I need to be right now. I fully accept myself as I am, where I am. I am capable, focused, and moving forward with purpose. I celebrate today's wins and welcome tomorrow's opportunities. I release judgment. I am worthy of everything I desire.

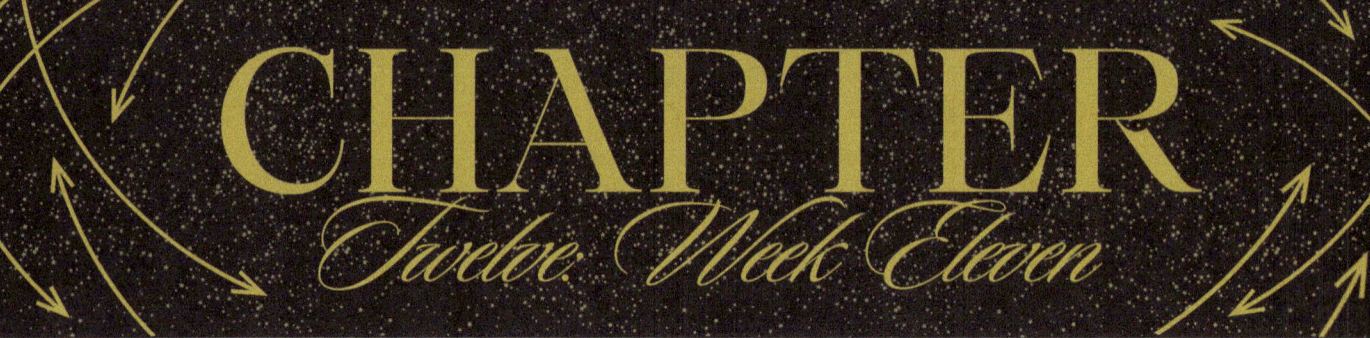

WEEKLY CHECK IN:

DATE: / /

LIST ANY SYNCHRONICITIES YOU NOTICE FROM LAST WEEK'S REFLECTION OR IN YOUR LIFE IN GENERAL:

LIST ANY CHANGES OR ADJUSTMENTS YOU NEED TO MAKE & WHY:

GOALS:

WITH THE ABOVE & THE INFORMATION YOU WROTE IN YOUR MONTHLY SECTION IN MIND, MAKE A LIST OF GOALS YOU WOULD LIKE TO ACCOMPLISH & WHY.

It may help to put your goal in this format: I want to accomplish_____ because _____.

FOR EACH OF THE GOALS LISTED, WRITE ONE OR MORE STEP(S) YOU CAN TAKE TO BRING YOU CLOSER TO REACHING EACH GOAL.

NOW PICK ONLY 3 TASKS ABOVE TO FOCUS ON THIS WEEK BY MARKING THEM WITH A STAR, HIGHLIGHTING, OR NUMBERING THEM.

Choose the three tasks that feel most aligned with your journey right now—whether that's what you're most intuitively drawn to, most excited about or what feels highest in priority. If priority is important to you this week, try numbering them from 1 to 3, with 1 being the most important. Choosing only three tasks at one time will keep the path forward clear and focused while limiting feelings of overwhelm.

Remember, if you finish these three tasks before the week is over, you can always come back to this page and take the next step. Use the extra space below if you need more room to organize your tasks or want to tackle a second group of tasks after completing the first this week.

MAKE A LIST OF HABITS YOU WOULD LIKE TO BUILD OR BREAK RIGHT NOW. THEN LIST HOW EACH WILL SUPPORT THE VERSION OF YOU THAT YOU DESIRE FOR YOURSELF.

It may help to put your habits in this format: I want to break/build_____habit, because _____.

Check In Day:

DATE: /   /

Take a moment to check in, connect with your body, and track your progression through reflection. Skip any sections that don't apply or that don't resonate. Answer each question by reflecting on your experiences, progress, and challenges since your last check-in. Note any changes or anything else that stands out to you.

Gratitude Practice:

List at least 3 things for which you are grateful and why.

_____

_____

_____

_____

Physical Check In:

HOW DO YOU FEEL PHYSICALLY RIGHT NOW?	**IN WHAT WAYS CAN YOU SUPPORT OR HONOR YOUR BODY AT THIS TIME?**

_____   _____

_____   _____

Emotional Check In:

HOW DO YOU FEEL EMOTIONALLY RIGHT NOW?	**What is contributing to how you feel Emotionally?**

_____

_____

LIST ANY REOCCURRING EMOTIONS YOU RECALL FEELING.	**What might these reoccurring feelings be telling you or what can you learn from them?**

_____

_____

WHAT ARE YOU DISAPPOINTED OR DISCONTENT WITH AND WHY?

_____

_____

_____

_____

_____

HOW CAN YOU RESOLVE, HEAL OR CHANGE WHAT YOU FEEL DISAPPOINTED OR DISCONTENT WITH? OR, HOW CAN YOU SUPPORT YOURSELF AT THIS TIME IF A RESOLUTION,CHANGE OR HEALING IS NOT POSSIBLE AT THIS TIME?

_____

_____

_____

_____

_____

WHAT BROUGHT YOU JOY, PEACE, CONTENTMENT AND/OR HAPPINESS?

WHAT DO YOU FEEL PROUD OF OR PROUD OF YOURSELF FOR?

_____

_____

_____

Mental Check In:

HOW DO YOU FEEL MENTALLY RIGHT NOW?

What is contributing to how you feel Mentally?

_____

_____

LIST ANY RECURRING THOUGHTS YOU RECALL HAVING.

_____

_____

_____

WHAT MIGHT THESE RECURRING THOUGHTS BE TELLING YOU? WHAT CAN YOU GLEAN FROM THEM?

_____

_____

_____

LIST ANY LIMITING BELIEFS OR LIMITING THOUGHTS YOU RECALL HAVING.

_____

_____

_____

HOW CAN YOU CHALLENGE OR REFRAME EACH OF THE ABOVE?

_____

_____

_____

Spiritual Check In:

HOW DO YOU FEEL SPIRITUALLY RIGHT NOW?

What is contributing to how you feel spiritually?

_____

_____

PROGRESSION THOUGH REFLECTION

WHAT DRAINED YOUR ENERGY ?

_____

_____

_____

_____

WHAT GAVE YOU ENERGY ?

_____

_____

_____

_____

Did you feel fully grounded and present?   ◯ Yes   ◯ No

If yes, what contributed to this feeling?

_____

If no, how can you foster more presence and ground yourself?

_____

Did you honor your boundaries?   ◯ Yes   ◯ No

If no, how can you better honor your boundaries moving forward?

_____

Did you honor your values and priorities?   ◯ Yes   ◯ No

If yes, how? Was it in the way you expected and if not, how did it differ from your expectations?

_____

If no, what got in the way and how can you better honor your values and priorities moving forward?

_____

HOW DID YOU NUTURE YOURSELF?
(Food, rest, movement, connection, spiritual practice, grounding, creativity, play, fun, other.)

_____

IS THERE ANYTHING YOU NEED RIGHT NOW THAT YOU ARE NOT GIVING YOURSELF?

_____

_____

Check in with your goals & progress:
DID YOU TAKE ANY STEPS TOWARDS ANY OF YOUR GOALS OR DO ANYTHING SMALL THAT ALIGNS WITH THE BIGGER VISION YOU HAVE FOR YOURSELF ?   ◯ Yes   ◯ No

If yes, how? If no, what got in the way and what can you do differently tomorrow?

_____

_____

LIST ANY GOALS THAT NEED MORE ATTENTION:

_____

_____

LIST A SMALL STEP YOU CAN TAKE TOMORROW TOWARDS EACH TO GET THE BALL ROLLING.

_____

_____

LOOK BACK AT THE HABITS YOU ARE WORKING TO BUILD OR BREAK IN YOUR WEEKLY REFLECTION. HOW DID YOU DO? WHERE DID YOU SHOW DISCIPLINE AND WHERE DID YOU DEFAULT?

_____

_____

_____

_____

IF YOU DEFAULTED BACK TO A HABIT YOU ARE TRYING TO BREAK, HOW CAN YOU REINFORCE YOUR WHY AND/OR MOVE FORWARD IN A MORE ALIGNED WAY? IS THERE A SMALLER STEP YOU CAN TAKE FIRST THAT WOULD MAKE THE TRANSITION EASIER OR FEEL LEST RESISTANT?

_____

_____

_____

_____

DID YOU LEARN ANYTHING NEW ABOUT YOURSELF, YOUR GOALS, THE WAY YOU TRACK PROGRESS OR SOMETHING ELSE? IF SO, WRITE IT DOWN BELOW.

_____

_____

_____

_____

USE THE SPACE BELOW FOR ANY ADDITIONAL NOTES:

TAKE A MOMENT TO AFFIRM THE FOLLOWING:
I am exactly where I need to be right now. I fully accept myself as I am, where I am. I am capable, focused, and moving forward with purpose. I celebrate today's wins and welcome tomorrow's opportunities. I release judgment. I am worthy of everything I desire.

Check In Day:

Take a moment to check in, connect with your body, and track your progression through reflection. Skip any sections that don't apply or that don't resonate. Answer each question by reflecting on your experiences, progress, and challenges since your last check-in. Note any changes or anything else that stands out to you.

Gratitude Practice:

List at least 3 things for which you are grateful and why.

_____

_____

_____

_____

Physical Check In:

HOW DO YOU FEEL PHYSICALLY RIGHT NOW?

IN WHAT WAYS CAN YOU SUPPORT OR HONOR YOUR BODY AT THIS TIME?

Emotional Check In:

HOW DO YOU FEEL EMOTIONALLY RIGHT NOW?

What is contributing to how you feel Emotionally?

LIST ANY REOCCURRING EMOTIONS YOU RECALL FEELING.

What might these reoccurring feelings be telling you or what can you learn from them?

WHAT ARE YOU DISAPPOINTED OR DISCONTENT WITH AND WHY?

_____

_____

_____

_____

_____

HOW CAN YOU RESOLVE, HEAL OR CHANGE WHAT YOU FEEL DISAPPOINTED OR DISCONTENT WITH? OR, HOW CAN YOU SUPPORT YOURSELF AT THIS TIME IF A RESOLUTION,CHANGE OR HEALING IS NOT POSSIBLE AT THIS TIME?

_____

_____

_____

_____

_____

WHAT BROUGHT YOU JOY, PEACE, CONTENTMENT AND/OR HAPPINESS?

WHAT DO YOU FEEL PROUD OF OR PROUD OF YOURSELF FOR?

_____

_____

_____

Mental Check In:

HOW DO YOU FEEL MENTALLY RIGHT NOW?

What is contributing to how you feel Mentally?

_____

_____

LIST ANY RECURRING THOUGHTS YOU RECALL HAVING.

_____

_____

_____

WHAT MIGHT THESE RECURRING THOUGHTS BE TELLING YOU? WHAT CAN YOU GLEAN FROM THEM?

_____

_____

_____

LIST ANY LIMITING BELIEFS OR LIMITING THOUGHTS YOU RECALL HAVING.

_____

_____

_____

HOW CAN YOU CHALLENGE OR REFRAME EACH OF THE ABOVE?

_____

_____

_____

Spiritual Check In:

HOW DO YOU FEEL SPIRITUALLY RIGHT NOW?

What is contributing to how you feel spiritually?

_____

_____

WHAT DRAINED YOUR ENERGY ?

_____

_____

_____

_____

WHAT GAVE YOU ENERGY ?

_____

_____

_____

_____

Did you feel fully grounded and present?   ◯ Yes   ◯ No

If yes, what contributed to this feeling?

_____

If no, how can you foster more presence and ground yourself?

_____

Did you honor your boundaries?   ◯ Yes   ◯ No

If no, how can you better honor your boundaries moving forward?

_____

Did you honor your values and priorities?   ◯ Yes   ◯ No

If yes, how? Was it in the way you expected and if not, how did it differ from your expectations?

_____

If no, what got in the way and how can you better honor your values and priorities moving forward?

_____

HOW DID YOU NUTURE YOURSELF?
(Food, rest, movement, connection, spiritual practice, grounding, creativity, play, fun, other.)

_____

IS THERE ANYTHING YOU NEED RIGHT NOW THAT YOU ARE NOT GIVING YOURSELF?

_____

_____

Check in with your goals & progress:

DID YOU TAKE ANY STEPS TOWARDS ANY OF YOUR GOALS OR DO ANYTHING SMALL THAT ALIGNS WITH THE BIGGER VISION YOU HAVE FOR YOURSELF ?   ◯ Yes   ◯ No

If yes, how? If no, what got in the way and what can you do differently tomorrow?

_____

_____

_____

LIST ANY GOALS THAT NEED MORE ATTENTION:

_____

_____

PROGRESSION THOUGH REFLECTION

LIST A SMALL STEP YOU CAN TAKE TOMORROW TOWARDS EACH TO GET THE BALL ROLLING.

_____

_____

LOOK BACK AT THE HABITS YOU ARE WORKING TO BUILD OR BREAK IN YOUR WEEKLY REFLECTION. HOW DID YOU DO? WHERE DID YOU SHOW DISCIPLINE AND WHERE DID YOU DEFAULT?

_____

_____

_____

_____

IF YOU DEFAULTED BACK TO A HABIT YOU ARE TRYING TO BREAK, HOW CAN YOU REINFORCE YOUR WHY AND/OR MOVE FORWARD IN A MORE ALIGNED WAY? IS THERE A SMALLER STEP YOU CAN TAKE FIRST THAT WOULD MAKE THE TRANSITION EASIER OR FEEL LEST RESISTANT?

_____

_____

_____

_____

DID YOU LEARN ANYTHING NEW ABOUT YOURSELF, YOUR GOALS, THE WAY YOU TRACK PROGRESS OR SOMETHING ELSE? IF SO, WRITE IT DOWN BELOW.

_____

_____

_____

_____

USE THE SPACE BELOW FOR ANY ADDITIONAL NOTES:

TAKE A MOMENT TO AFFIRM THE FOLLOWING:
I am exactly where I need to be right now. I fully accept myself as I am, where I am. I am capable, focused, and moving forward with purpose. I celebrate today's wins and welcome tomorrow's opportunities. I release judgment. I am worthy of everything I desire.

Check In Day:

DATE: / /

Take a moment to check in, connect with your body, and track your progression through reflection. Skip any sections that don't apply or that don't resonate. Answer each question by reflecting on your experiences, progress, and challenges since your last check-in. Note any changes or anything else that stands out to you.

Gratitude Practice:

List at least 3 things for which you are grateful and why.

_____

_____

_____

_____

Physical Check In:

HOW DO YOU FEEL PHYSICALLY RIGHT NOW?

IN WHAT WAYS CAN YOU SUPPORT OR HONOR YOUR BODY AT THIS TIME?

_____

_____

Emotional Check In:

HOW DO YOU FEEL EMOTIONALLY RIGHT NOW?

What is contributing to how you feel Emotionally?

_____

_____

LIST ANY REOCCURRING EMOTIONS YOU RECALL FEELING.

What might these reoccurring feelings be telling you or what can you learn from them?

_____

_____

191

PROGRESSION THOUGH REFLECTION

WHAT ARE YOU DISAPPOINTED OR DISCONTENT WITH AND WHY?

_____

_____

_____

_____

_____

HOW CAN YOU RESOLVE, HEAL OR CHANGE WHAT YOU FEEL DISAPPOINTED OR DISCONTENT WITH? OR, HOW CAN YOU SUPPORT YOURSELF AT THIS TIME IF A RESOLUTION,CHANGE OR HEALING IS NOT POSSIBLE AT THIS TIME?

_____

_____

_____

_____

_____

WHAT BROUGHT YOU JOY, PEACE, CONTENTMENT AND/OR HAPPINESS?

WHAT DO YOU FEEL PROUD OF OR PROUD OF YOURSELF FOR?

_____

_____

_____

Mental Check In:

| HOW DO YOU FEEL MENTALLY RIGHT NOW? |

What is contributing to how you feel Mentally?

_____

_____

LIST ANY RECURRING THOUGHTS YOU RECALL HAVING.

_____

_____

_____

WHAT MIGHT THESE RECURRING THOUGHTS BE TELLING YOU? WHAT CAN YOU GLEAN FROM THEM?

_____

_____

_____

LIST ANY LIMITING BELIEFS OR LIMITING THOUGHTS YOU RECALL HAVING.

_____

_____

_____

HOW CAN YOU CHALLENGE OR REFRAME EACH OF THE ABOVE?

_____

_____

_____

Spiritual Check In:

HOW DO YOU FEEL SPIRITUALLY RIGHT NOW?

What is contributing to how you feel spiritually?

_____

_____

PROGRESSION THOUGH REFLECTION

WHAT DRAINED YOUR ENERGY ?

_____

_____

_____

_____

Did you feel fully grounded and present?   ◯ Yes   ◯ No

If yes, what contributed to this feeling?

If no, how can you foster more presence and ground yourself?

Did you honor your boundaries?   ◯ Yes   ◯ No

If no, how can you better honor your boundaries moving forward?

Did you honor your values and priorities?   ◯ Yes   ◯ No

If yes, how? Was it in the way you expected and if not, how did it differ from your expectations?

If no, what got in the way and how can you better honor your values and priorities moving forward?

HOW DID YOU NUTURE YOURSELF?
(Food, rest, movement, connection, spiritual practice, grounding, creativity, play, fun, other.)

IS THERE ANYTHING YOU NEED RIGHT NOW THAT YOU ARE NOT GIVING YOURSELF?

_____

_____

WHAT GAVE YOU ENERGY ?

_____

_____

_____

_____

Check in with your goals & progress:
DID YOU TAKE ANY STEPS TOWARDS ANY OF YOUR GOALS OR DO ANYTHING SMALL THAT ALIGNS WITH THE BIGGER VISION YOU HAVE FOR YOURSELF ?   ◯ Yes   ◯ No

If yes, how? If no, what got in the way and what can you do differently tomorrow?

_____

_____

LIST ANY GOALS THAT NEED MORE ATTENTION:

_____

_____

LIST A SMALL STEP YOU CAN TAKE TOMORROW TOWARDS EACH TO GET THE BALL ROLLING.

_____

_____

LOOK BACK AT THE HABITS YOU ARE WORKING TO BUILD OR BREAK IN YOUR WEEKLY REFLECTION. HOW DID YOU DO? WHERE DID YOU SHOW DISCIPLINE AND WHERE DID YOU DEFAULT?

_____

_____

_____

IF YOU DEFAULTED BACK TO A HABIT YOU ARE TRYING TO BREAK, HOW CAN YOU REINFORCE YOUR WHY AND/OR MOVE FORWARD IN A MORE ALIGNED WAY? IS THERE A SMALLER STEP YOU CAN TAKE FIRST THAT WOULD MAKE THE TRANSITION EASIER OR FEEL LEST RESISTANT?

_____

_____

_____

_____

DID YOU LEARN ANYTHING NEW ABOUT YOURSELF, YOUR GOALS, THE WAY YOU TRACK PROGRESS OR SOMETHING ELSE? IF SO, WRITE IT DOWN BELOW.

_____

_____

_____

_____

USE THE SPACE BELOW FOR ANY ADDITIONAL NOTES:

TAKE A MOMENT TO AFFIRM THE FOLLOWING:
I am exactly where I need to be right now. I fully accept myself as I am, where I am. I am capable, focused, and moving forward with purpose. I celebrate today's wins and welcome tomorrow's opportunities. I release judgment. I am worthy of everything I desire.

CHAPTER
Thirteen: Week Twelve

WEEKLY CHECK IN:

LIST ANY SYNCHRONICITIES YOU NOTICE FROM LAST WEEK'S REFLECTION OR IN YOUR LIFE IN GENERAL:

LIST ANY CHANGES OR ADJUSTMENTS YOU NEED TO MAKE & WHY:

GOALS:

WITH THE ABOVE & THE INFORMATION YOU WROTE IN YOUR MONTHLY SECTION IN MIND, MAKE A LIST OF GOALS YOU WOULD LIKE TO ACCOMPLISH & WHY.

It may help to put your goal in this format: I want to accomplish_____ because _____.

PROGRESSION THOUGH REFLECTION

FOR EACH OF THE GOALS LISTED, WRITE ONE OR MORE STEP(S) YOU CAN TAKE TO BRING YOU CLOSER TO REACHING EACH GOAL.

NOW PICK ONLY 3 TASKS ABOVE TO FOCUS ON THIS WEEK BY MARKING THEM WITH A STAR, HIGHLIGHTING, OR NUMBERING THEM.

Choose the three tasks that feel most aligned with your journey right now—whether that's what you're most intuitively drawn to, most excited about or what feels highest in priority. If priority is important to you this week, try numbering them from 1 to 3, with 1 being the most important. Choosing only three tasks at one time will keep the path forward clear and focused while limiting feelings of overwhelm.

Remember, if you finish these three tasks before the week is over, you can always come back to this page and take the next step. Use the extra space below if you need more room to organize your tasks or want to tackle a second group of tasks after completing the first this week.

MAKE A LIST OF HABITS YOU WOULD LIKE TO BUILD OR BREAK RIGHT NOW. THEN LIST HOW EACH WILL SUPPORT THE VERSION OF YOU THAT YOU DESIRE FOR YOURSELF.

It may help to put your habits in this format: I want to break/build_____habit, because _____.

Check In Day:

Take a moment to check in, connect with your body, and track your progression through reflection. Skip any sections that don't apply or that don't resonate. Answer each question by reflecting on your experiences, progress, and challenges since your last check-in. Note any changes or anything else that stands out to you.

Gratitude Practice:

List at least 3 things for which you are grateful and why.

_____

_____

_____

_____

Physical Check In:

HOW DO YOU FEEL PHYSICALLY RIGHT NOW?

IN WHAT WAYS CAN YOU SUPPORT OR HONOR YOUR BODY AT THIS TIME?

_____   _____

_____   _____

Emotional Check In:

HOW DO YOU FEEL EMOTIONALLY RIGHT NOW?

What is contributing to how you feel Emotionally?

_____

_____

LIST ANY REOCCURRING EMOTIONS YOU RECALL FEELING.

What might these reoccurring feelings be telling you or what can you learn from them?

_____

_____

WHAT ARE YOU DISAPPOINTED OR DISCONTENT WITH AND WHY?

_____

_____

_____

_____

_____

HOW CAN YOU RESOLVE, HEAL OR CHANGE WHAT YOU FEEL DISAPPOINTED OR DISCONTENT WITH? OR, HOW CAN YOU SUPPORT YOURSELF AT THIS TIME IF A RESOLUTION,CHANGE OR HEALING IS NOT POSSIBLE AT THIS TIME?

_____

_____

_____

_____

_____

WHAT BROUGHT YOU JOY, PEACE, CONTENTMENT AND/OR HAPPINESS?

WHAT DO YOU FEEL PROUD OF OR PROUD OF YOURSELF FOR?

_____

_____

_____

Mental Check In:

HOW DO YOU FEEL MENTALLY RIGHT NOW?

What is contributing to how you feel Mentally?

_____

_____

LIST ANY RECURRING THOUGHTS YOU RECALL HAVING.

_____

_____

_____

WHAT MIGHT THESE RECURRING THOUGHTS BE TELLING YOU? WHAT CAN YOU GLEAN FROM THEM?

_____

_____

_____

LIST ANY LIMITING BELIEFS OR LIMITING THOUGHTS YOU RECALL HAVING.

_____

_____

_____

HOW CAN YOU CHALLENGE OR REFRAME EACH OF THE ABOVE?

_____

_____

_____

Spiritual Check In:

HOW DO YOU FEEL SPIRITUALLY RIGHT NOW?

What is contributing to how you feel spiritually?

_____

_____

200

WHAT DRAINED YOUR ENERGY ?

_____

_____

_____

WHAT GAVE YOU ENERGY ?

_____

_____

_____

Did you feel fully grounded and present?   ◯ Yes   ◯ No

If yes, what contributed to this feeling?

_____

If no, how can you foster more presence and ground yourself?

_____

Did you honor your boundaries?   ◯ Yes   ◯ No

If no, how can you better honor your boundaries moving forward?

_____

Did you honor your values and priorities?   ◯ Yes   ◯ No

If yes, how? Was it in the way you expected and if not, how did it differ from your expectations?

_____

If no, what got in the way and how can you better honor your values and priorities moving forward?

_____

HOW DID YOU NUTURE YOURSELF?

(Food, rest, movement, connection, spiritual practice, grounding, creativity, play, fun, other.)

_____

IS THERE ANYTHING YOU NEED RIGHT NOW THAT YOU ARE NOT GIVING YOURSELF?

_____

_____

Check in with your goals & progress:

DID YOU TAKE ANY STEPS TOWARDS ANY OF YOUR GOALS OR DO ANYTHING SMALL THAT ALIGNS WITH THE BIGGER VISION YOU HAVE FOR YOURSELF ?   ◯ Yes ◯ No

If yes, how? If no, what got in the way and what can you do differently tomorrow?

_____

_____

LIST ANY GOALS THAT NEED MORE ATTENTION:

_____

_____

PROGRESSION THOUGH REFLECTION

LIST A SMALL STEP YOU CAN TAKE TOMORROW TOWARDS EACH TO GET THE BALL ROLLING.

_____

_____

LOOK BACK AT THE HABITS YOU ARE WORKING TO BUILD OR BREAK IN YOUR WEEKLY REFLECTION. HOW DID YOU DO? WHERE DID YOU SHOW DISCIPLINE AND WHERE DID YOU DEFAULT?

_____

_____

_____

_____

IF YOU DEFAULTED BACK TO A HABIT YOU ARE TRYING TO BREAK, HOW CAN YOU REINFORCE YOUR WHY AND/OR MOVE FORWARD IN A MORE ALIGNED WAY? IS THERE A SMALLER STEP YOU CAN TAKE FIRST THAT WOULD MAKE THE TRANSITION EASIER OR FEEL LEST RESISTANT?

_____

_____

_____

_____

DID YOU LEARN ANYTHING NEW ABOUT YOURSELF, YOUR GOALS, THE WAY YOU TRACK PROGRESS OR SOMETHING ELSE? IF SO, WRITE IT DOWN BELOW.

_____

_____

_____

_____

USE THE SPACE BELOW FOR ANY ADDITIONAL NOTES:

TAKE A MOMENT TO AFFIRM THE FOLLOWING:
I am exactly where I need to be right now. I fully accept myself as I am, where I am. I am capable, focused, and moving forward with purpose. I celebrate today's wins and welcome tomorrow's opportunities. I release judgment. I am worthy of everything I desire.

Check In Day:

DATE: / /

Take a moment to check in, connect with your body, and track your progression through reflection. Skip any sections that don't apply or that don't resonate. Answer each question by reflecting on your experiences, progress, and challenges since your last check-in. Note any changes or anything else that stands out to you.

Gratitude Practice:

List at least 3 things for which you are grateful and why.

_____

_____

_____

_____

Physical Check In:

HOW DO YOU FEEL PHYSICALLY RIGHT NOW?

IN WHAT WAYS CAN YOU SUPPORT OR HONOR YOUR BODY AT THIS TIME?

_____   _____

_____   _____

Emotional Check In:

HOW DO YOU FEEL EMOTIONALLY RIGHT NOW?

What is contributing to how you feel Emotionally?

_____

_____

LIST ANY REOCCURRING EMOTIONS YOU RECALL FEELING.

What might these reoccurring feelings be telling you or what can you learn from them?

_____

_____

PROGRESSION THOUGH REFLECTION

WHAT ARE YOU DISAPPOINTED OR DISCONTENT WITH AND WHY?

_____

_____

_____

_____

_____

HOW CAN YOU RESOLVE, HEAL OR CHANGE WHAT YOU FEEL DISAPPOINTED OR DISCONTENT WITH? OR, HOW CAN YOU SUPPORT YOURSELF AT THIS TIME IF A RESOLUTION, CHANGE OR HEALING IS NOT POSSIBLE AT THIS TIME?

_____

_____

_____

_____

_____

WHAT BROUGHT YOU JOY, PEACE, CONTENTMENT AND/OR HAPPINESS?

WHAT DO YOU FEEL PROUD OF OR PROUD OF YOURSELF FOR?

_____

_____

_____

Mental Check In:

HOW DO YOU FEEL MENTALLY RIGHT NOW?

What is contributing to how you feel Mentally?

_____

_____

LIST ANY RECURRING THOUGHTS YOU RECALL HAVING.

_____

_____

_____

WHAT MIGHT THESE RECURRING THOUGHTS BE TELLING YOU? WHAT CAN YOU GLEAN FROM THEM?

_____

_____

_____

LIST ANY LIMITING BELIEFS OR LIMITING THOUGHTS YOU RECALL HAVING.

_____

_____

_____

HOW CAN YOU CHALLENGE OR REFRAME EACH OF THE ABOVE?

_____

_____

_____

Spiritual Check In:

HOW DO YOU FEEL SPIRITUALLY RIGHT NOW?

What is contributing to how you feel spiritually?

_____

_____

PROGRESSION THOUGH REFLECTION

WHAT DRAINED YOUR ENERGY ?

_____

_____

_____

_____

WHAT GAVE YOU ENERGY ?

_____

_____

_____

_____

Did you feel fully grounded and present?   ◯ Yes   ◯ No
If yes, what contributed to this feeling?

_____

If no, how can you foster more presence and ground yourself?

_____

Did you honor your boundaries?   ◯ Yes   ◯ No
If no, how can you better honor your boundaries moving forward?

_____

Did you honor your values and priorities?   ◯ Yes   ◯ No
If yes, how? Was it in the way you expected and if not, how did it differ from your expectations?

_____

If no, what got in the way and how can you better honor your values and priorities moving forward?

_____

HOW DID YOU NUTURE YOURSELF?
(Food, rest, movement, connection, spiritual practice, grounding, creativity, play, fun, other.)

_____

IS THERE ANYTHING YOU NEED RIGHT NOW THAT YOU ARE NOT GIVING YOURSELF?

_____

_____

Check in with your goals & progress:
DID YOU TAKE ANY STEPS TOWARDS ANY OF YOUR GOALS OR DO ANYTHING SMALL THAT ALIGNS WITH THE BIGGER VISION YOU HAVE FOR YOURSELF ?   ◯ Yes   ◯ No
If yes, how? If no, what got in the way and what can you do differently tomorrow?

_____

_____

_____

LIST ANY GOALS THAT NEED MORE ATTENTION:

_____

_____

LIST A SMALL STEP YOU CAN TAKE TOMORROW TOWARDS EACH TO GET THE BALL ROLLING.

_____

_____

LOOK BACK AT THE HABITS YOU ARE WORKING TO BUILD OR BREAK IN YOUR WEEKLY REFLECTION. HOW DID YOU DO? WHERE DID YOU SHOW DISCIPLINE AND WHERE DID YOU DEFAULT?

_____

_____

_____

IF YOU DEFAULTED BACK TO A HABIT YOU ARE TRYING TO BREAK, HOW CAN YOU REINFORCE YOUR WHY AND/OR MOVE FORWARD IN A MORE ALIGNED WAY? IS THERE A SMALLER STEP YOU CAN TAKE FIRST THAT WOULD MAKE THE TRANSITION EASIER OR FEEL LEST RESISTANT?

_____

_____

_____

DID YOU LEARN ANYTHING NEW ABOUT YOURSELF, YOUR GOALS, THE WAY YOU TRACK PROGRESS OR SOMETHING ELSE? IF SO, WRITE IT DOWN BELOW.

_____

_____

_____

USE THE SPACE BELOW FOR ANY ADDITIONAL NOTES:

TAKE A MOMENT TO AFFIRM THE FOLLOWING:
I am exactly where I need to be right now. I fully accept myself as I am, where I am. I am capable, focused, and moving forward with purpose. I celebrate today's wins and welcome tomorrow's opportunities. I release judgment. I am worthy of everything I desire.

Check In Day:

DATE: / /

Take a moment to check in, connect with your body, and track your progression through reflection. Skip any sections that don't apply or that don't resonate. Answer each question by reflecting on your experiences, progress, and challenges since your last check-in. Note any changes or anything else that stands out to you.

Gratitude Practice:

List at least 3 things for which you are grateful and why.

_____

_____

_____

_____

Physical Check In:

HOW DO YOU FEEL PHYSICALLY RIGHT NOW?

IN WHAT WAYS CAN YOU SUPPORT OR HONOR YOUR BODY AT THIS TIME?

Emotional Check In:

HOW DO YOU FEEL EMOTIONALLY RIGHT NOW?

What is contributing to how you feel Emotionally?

LIST ANY REOCCURRING EMOTIONS YOU RECALL FEELING.

What might these reoccurring feelings be telling you or what can you learn from them?

WHAT ARE YOU DISAPPOINTED OR DISCONTENT WITH AND WHY?

_____

_____

_____

_____

_____

HOW CAN YOU RESOLVE, HEAL OR CHANGE WHAT YOU FEEL DISAPPOINTED OR DISCONTENT WITH? OR, HOW CAN YOU SUPPORT YOURSELF AT THIS TIME IF A RESOLUTION,CHANGE OR HEALING IS NOT POSSIBLE AT THIS TIME?

_____

_____

_____

_____

_____

WHAT BROUGHT YOU JOY, PEACE, CONTENTMENT AND/OR HAPPINESS?

WHAT DO YOU FEEL PROUD OF OR PROUD OF YOURSELF FOR?

_____

_____

_____

Mental Check In:

HOW DO YOU FEEL MENTALLY RIGHT NOW?

What is contributing to how you feel Mentally?

_____

_____

LIST ANY RECURRING THOUGHTS YOU RECALL HAVING.

_____

_____

_____

WHAT MIGHT THESE RECURRING THOUGHTS BE TELLING YOU? WHAT CAN YOU GLEAN FROM THEM?

_____

_____

_____

LIST ANY LIMITING BELIEFS OR LIMITING THOUGHTS YOU RECALL HAVING.

_____

_____

HOW CAN YOU CHALLENGE OR REFRAME EACH OF THE ABOVE?

_____

_____

_____

Spiritual Check In:

HOW DO YOU FEEL SPIRITUALLY RIGHT NOW?

What is contributing to how you feel spiritually?

_____

_____

WHAT DRAINED YOUR ENERGY ?

WHAT GAVE YOU ENERGY ?

_____

_____

_____

_____

Did you feel fully grounded and present?   ◯ Yes   ◯ No

If yes, what contributed to this feeling?

_____

If no, how can you foster more presence and ground yourself?

_____

Did you honor your boundaries?   ◯ Yes   ◯ No

If no, how can you better honor your boundaries moving forward?

_____

Did you honor your values and priorities?   ◯ Yes   ◯ No

If yes, how? Was it in the way you expected and if not, how did it differ from your expectations?

_____

If no, what got in the way and how can you better honor your values and priorities moving forward?

_____

HOW DID YOU NUTURE YOURSELF?
(Food, rest, movement, connection, spiritual practice, grounding, creativity, play, fun, other.)

_____

IS THERE ANYTHING YOU NEED RIGHT NOW THAT YOU ARE NOT GIVING YOURSELF?

_____

_____

Check in with your goals & progress:

DID YOU TAKE ANY STEPS TOWARDS ANY OF YOUR GOALS OR DO ANYTHING SMALL THAT ALIGNS WITH THE BIGGER VISION YOU HAVE FOR YOURSELF ?   ◯ Yes   ◯ No

If yes, how? If no, what got in the way and what can you do differently tomorrow?

_____

_____

_____

LIST ANY GOALS THAT NEED MORE ATTENTION:

_____

_____

LIST A SMALL STEP YOU CAN TAKE TOMORROW TOWARDS EACH TO GET THE BALL ROLLING.

_____

_____

LOOK BACK AT THE HABITS YOU ARE WORKING TO BUILD OR BREAK IN YOUR WEEKLY REFLECTION. HOW DID YOU DO? WHERE DID YOU SHOW DISCIPLINE AND WHERE DID YOU DEFAULT?

_____

_____

_____

_____

IF YOU DEFAULTED BACK TO A HABIT YOU ARE TRYING TO BREAK, HOW CAN YOU REINFORCE YOUR WHY AND/OR MOVE FORWARD IN A MORE ALIGNED WAY? IS THERE A SMALLER STEP YOU CAN TAKE FIRST THAT WOULD MAKE THE TRANSITION EASIER OR FEEL LEST RESISTANT?

_____

_____

_____

_____

DID YOU LEARN ANYTHING NEW ABOUT YOURSELF, YOUR GOALS, THE WAY YOU TRACK PROGRESS OR SOMETHING ELSE? IF SO, WRITE IT DOWN BELOW.

_____

_____

_____

_____

USE THE SPACE BELOW FOR ANY ADDITIONAL NOTES:

TAKE A MOMENT TO AFFIRM THE FOLLOWING:
I am exactly where I need to be right now. I fully accept myself as I am, where I am. I am capable, focused, and moving forward with purpose. I celebrate today's wins and welcome tomorrow's opportunities. I release judgment. I am worthy of everything I desire.

FINAL WEEKLY CHECK IN:

DATE: / /

LIST ANY SYNCHRONICITIES YOU NOTICE FROM LAST WEEK'S REFLECTION OR IN YOUR LIFE IN GENERAL:

LIST ANY CHANGES OR ADJUSTMENTS YOU NEED TO MAKE & WHY:

GOALS:

WITH THE ABOVE & THE INFORMATION YOU WROTE IN YOUR MONTHLY SECTION IN MIND, MAKE A LIST OF GOALS YOU WOULD LIKE TO ACCOMPLISH & WHY.

It may help to put your goal in this format: I want to accomplish_____ because _____.

FOR EACH OF THE GOALS LISTED, WRITE ONE OR MORE STEP(S) YOU CAN TAKE TO BRING YOU CLOSER TO REACHING EACH GOAL.

NOW PICK ONLY 3 TASKS ABOVE TO FOCUS ON THIS WEEK BY MARKING THEM WITH A STAR, HIGHLIGHTING, OR NUMBERING THEM.

Choose the three tasks that feel most aligned with your journey right now—whether that's what you're most intuitively drawn to, most excited about or what feels highest in priority. If priority is important to you this week, try numbering them from 1 to 3, with 1 being the most important. Choosing only three tasks at one time will keep the path forward clear and focused while limiting feelings of overwhelm.

Remember, if you finish these three tasks before the week is over, you can always come back to this page and take the next step. Use the extra space below if you need more room to organize your tasks or want to tackle a second group of tasks after completing the first this week.

MAKE A LIST OF HABITS YOU WOULD LIKE TO BUILD OR BREAK RIGHT NOW. THEN LIST HOW EACH WILL SUPPORT THE VERSION OF YOU THAT YOU DESIRE FOR YOURSELF.

It may help to put your habits in this format: I want to break/build_____habit, because _____.

Check In Day:

DATE: / /

Take a moment to check in, connect with your body, and track your progression through reflection. Skip any sections that don't apply or that don't resonate. Answer each question by reflecting on your experiences, progress, and challenges since your last check-in. Note any changes or anything else that stands out to you.

Gratitude Practice:

List at least 3 things for which you are grateful and why.

_____

_____

_____

_____

Physical Check In:

HOW DO YOU FEEL PHYSICALLY RIGHT NOW?

IN WHAT WAYS CAN YOU SUPPORT OR HONOR YOUR BODY AT THIS TIME?

_____   _____

_____   _____

Emotional Check In:

HOW DO YOU FEEL EMOTIONALLY RIGHT NOW?

What is contributing to how you feel Emotionally?

_____

_____

LIST ANY REOCCURRING EMOTIONS YOU RECALL FEELING.

What might these reoccurring feelings be telling you or what can you learn from them?

_____

_____

PROGRESSION THOUGH REFLECTION

WHAT ARE YOU DISAPPOINTED OR DISCONTENT WITH AND WHY?

_____

_____

_____

_____

_____

HOW CAN YOU RESOLVE, HEAL OR CHANGE WHAT YOU FEEL DISAPPOINTED OR DISCONTENT WITH? OR, HOW CAN YOU SUPPORT YOURSELF AT THIS TIME IF A RESOLUTION, CHANGE OR HEALING IS NOT POSSIBLE AT THIS TIME?

_____

_____

_____

_____

_____

WHAT BROUGHT YOU JOY, PEACE, CONTENTMENT AND/OR HAPPINESS?

WHAT DO YOU FEEL PROUD OF OR PROUD OF YOURSELF FOR?

_____

_____

_____

Mental Check In:

HOW DO YOU FEEL MENTALLY RIGHT NOW?

What is contributing to how you feel Mentally?

_____

_____

LIST ANY RECURRING THOUGHTS YOU RECALL HAVING.

_____

_____

_____

WHAT MIGHT THESE RECURRING THOUGHTS BE TELLING YOU? WHAT CAN YOU GLEAN FROM THEM?

_____

_____

_____

LIST ANY LIMITING BELIEFS OR LIMITING THOUGHTS YOU RECALL HAVING.

_____

_____

_____

HOW CAN YOU CHALLENGE OR REFRAME EACH OF THE ABOVE?

_____

_____

_____

Spiritual Check In:

HOW DO YOU FEEL SPIRITUALLY RIGHT NOW?

What is contributing to how you feel spiritually?

_____

_____

PROGRESSION THOUGH REFLECTION

WHAT DRAINED YOUR ENERGY ?

WHAT GAVE YOU ENERGY ?

_____

_____

_____

_____

_____

_____

_____

_____

Did you feel fully grounded and present?   ◯ Yes   ◯ No

If yes, what contributed to this feeling?

If no, how can you foster more presence and ground yourself?

Did you honor your boundaries?   ◯ Yes   ◯ No

If no, how can you better honor your boundaries moving forward?

Did you honor your values and priorities?   ◯ Yes   ◯ No

If yes, how? Was it in the way you expected and if not, how did it differ from your expectations?

If no, what got in the way and how can you better honor your values and priorities moving forward?

HOW DID YOU NUTURE YOURSELF?
(Food, rest, movement, connection, spiritual practice, grounding, creativity, play, fun, other.)

IS THERE ANYTHING YOU NEED RIGHT NOW THAT YOU ARE NOT GIVING YOURSELF?

_____

_____

Check in with your goals & progress:

DID YOU TAKE ANY STEPS TOWARDS ANY OF YOUR GOALS OR DO ANYTHING SMALL THAT ALIGNS WITH THE BIGGER VISION YOU HAVE FOR YOURSELF ?   ◯ Yes ◯ No

If yes, how? If no, what got in the way and what can you do differently tomorrow?

_____

_____

_____

LIST ANY GOALS THAT NEED MORE ATTENTION:

_____

_____

LIST A SMALL STEP YOU CAN TAKE TOMORROW TOWARDS EACH TO GET THE BALL ROLLING.

_____

_____

LOOK BACK AT THE HABITS YOU ARE WORKING TO BUILD OR BREAK IN YOUR WEEKLY REFLECTION. HOW DID YOU DO? WHERE DID YOU SHOW DISCIPLINE AND WHERE DID YOU DEFAULT?

_____

_____

_____

IF YOU DEFAULTED BACK TO A HABIT YOU ARE TRYING TO BREAK, HOW CAN YOU REINFORCE YOUR WHY AND/OR MOVE FORWARD IN A MORE ALIGNED WAY? IS THERE A SMALLER STEP YOU CAN TAKE FIRST THAT WOULD MAKE THE TRANSITION EASIER OR FEEL LEST RESISTANT?

_____

_____

_____

DID YOU LEARN ANYTHING NEW ABOUT YOURSELF, YOUR GOALS, THE WAY YOU TRACK PROGRESS OR SOMETHING ELSE? IF SO, WRITE IT DOWN BELOW.

_____

_____

_____

USE THE SPACE BELOW FOR ANY ADDITIONAL NOTES:

<u>TAKE A MOMENT TO AFFIRM THE FOLLOWING:</u>
I am exactly where I need to be right now. I fully accept myself as I am, where I am. I am capable, focused, and moving forward with purpose. I celebrate today's wins and welcome tomorrow's opportunities. I release judgment. I am worthy of everything I desire.

Check In Day:

DATE: / /

Take a moment to check in, connect with your body, and track your progression through reflection. Skip any sections that don't apply or that don't resonate. Answer each question by reflecting on your experiences, progress, and challenges since your last check-in. Note any changes or anything else that stands out to you.

Gratitude Practice:

List at least 3 things for which you are grateful and why.

_____

_____

_____

_____

Physical Check In:

HOW DO YOU FEEL PHYSICALLY RIGHT NOW?

IN WHAT WAYS CAN YOU SUPPORT OR HONOR YOUR BODY AT THIS TIME?

_____

_____

Emotional Check In:

HOW DO YOU FEEL EMOTIONALLY RIGHT NOW?

What is contributing to how you feel Emotionally?

_____

LIST ANY REOCCURRING EMOTIONS YOU RECALL FEELING.

What might these reoccurring feelings be telling you or what can you learn from them?

_____

220

WHAT ARE YOU DISAPPOINTED OR DISCONTENT WITH AND WHY?

_____

_____

_____

_____

_____

HOW CAN YOU RESOLVE, HEAL OR CHANGE WHAT YOU FEEL DISAPPOINTED OR DISCONTENT WITH? OR, HOW CAN YOU SUPPORT YOURSELF AT THIS TIME IF A RESOLUTION,CHANGE OR HEALING IS NOT POSSIBLE AT THIS TIME?

_____

_____

_____

_____

_____

WHAT BROUGHT YOU JOY, PEACE, CONTENTMENT AND/OR HAPPINESS?

WHAT DO YOU FEEL PROUD OF OR PROUD OF YOURSELF FOR?

_____

_____

_____

Mental Check In:

| HOW DO YOU FEEL MENTALLY RIGHT NOW? |

What is contributing to how you feel Mentally?

_____

_____

LIST ANY RECURRING THOUGHTS YOU RECALL HAVING.

_____

_____

_____

WHAT MIGHT THESE RECURRING THOUGHTS BE TELLING YOU? WHAT CAN YOU GLEAN FROM THEM?

_____

_____

_____

LIST ANY LIMITING BELIEFS OR LIMITING THOUGHTS YOU RECALL HAVING.

_____

_____

_____

HOW CAN YOU CHALLENGE OR REFRAME EACH OF THE ABOVE?

_____

_____

_____

Spiritual Check In:

HOW DO YOU FEEL SPIRITUALLY RIGHT NOW?

What is contributing to how you feel spiritually?

_____

_____

WHAT DRAINED YOUR ENERGY ?

_____

_____

_____

Did you feel fully grounded and present?   ◯ Yes   ◯ No

If yes, what contributed to this feeling?

_____

If no, how can you foster more presence and ground yourself?

_____

Did you honor your boundaries?   ◯ Yes   ◯ No

If no, how can you better honor your boundaries moving forward?

_____

Did you honor your values and priorities?   ◯ Yes   ◯ No

If yes, how? Was it in the way you expected and if not, how did it differ from your expectations?

_____

If no, what got in the way and how can you better honor your values and priorities moving forward?

_____

WHAT GAVE YOU ENERGY ?

_____

_____

_____

HOW DID YOU NUTURE YOURSELF?

(Food, rest, movement, connection, spiritual practice, grounding, creativity, play, fun, other.)

_____

IS THERE ANYTHING YOU NEED RIGHT NOW THAT YOU ARE NOT GIVING YOURSELF?

_____

_____

Check in with your goals & progress:

DID YOU TAKE ANY STEPS TOWARDS ANY OF YOUR GOALS OR DO ANYTHING SMALL THAT ALIGNS WITH THE BIGGER VISION YOU HAVE FOR YOURSELF ?   ◯ Yes   ◯ No

If yes, how? If no, what got in the way and what can you do differently tomorrow?

_____

_____

LIST ANY GOALS THAT NEED MORE ATTENTION:

_____

_____

LIST A SMALL STEP YOU CAN TAKE TOMORROW TOWARDS EACH TO GET THE BALL ROLLING.

_____

_____

LOOK BACK AT THE HABITS YOU ARE WORKING TO BUILD OR BREAK IN YOUR WEEKLY REFLECTION. HOW DID YOU DO? WHERE DID YOU SHOW DISCIPLINE AND WHERE DID YOU DEFAULT?

_____

_____

_____

_____

IF YOU DEFAULTED BACK TO A HABIT YOU ARE TRYING TO BREAK, HOW CAN YOU REINFORCE YOUR WHY AND/OR MOVE FORWARD IN A MORE ALIGNED WAY? IS THERE A SMALLER STEP YOU CAN TAKE FIRST THAT WOULD MAKE THE TRANSITION EASIER OR FEEL LEST RESISTANT?

_____

_____

_____

_____

DID YOU LEARN ANYTHING NEW ABOUT YOURSELF, YOUR GOALS, THE WAY YOU TRACK PROGRESS OR SOMETHING ELSE? IF SO, WRITE IT DOWN BELOW.

_____

_____

_____

_____

USE THE SPACE BELOW FOR ANY ADDITIONAL NOTES:

TAKE A MOMENT TO AFFIRM THE FOLLOWING:
I am exactly where I need to be right now. I fully accept myself as I am, where I am. I am capable, focused, and moving forward with purpose. I celebrate today's wins and welcome tomorrow's opportunities. I release judgment. I am worthy of everything I desire.

Final Check In Day:

Take a moment to check in, connect with your body, and track your progression through reflection. Skip any sections that don't apply or that don't resonate. Answer each question by reflecting on your experiences, progress, and challenges since your last check-in. Note any changes or anything else that stands out to you.

Gratitude Practice:

List at least 3 things for which you are grateful and why.

_____

_____

_____

_____

Physical Check In:

HOW DO YOU FEEL PHYSICALLY RIGHT NOW?	IN WHAT WAYS CAN YOU SUPPORT OR HONOR YOUR BODY AT THIS TIME?

_____   _____

_____   _____

Emotional Check In:

HOW DO YOU FEEL EMOTIONALLY RIGHT NOW?	What is contributing to how you feel Emotionally?

_____

_____

LIST ANY REOCCURRING EMOTIONS YOU RECALL FEELING.	What might these reoccurring feelings be telling you or what can you learn from them?

_____

_____

225

WHAT ARE YOU DISAPPOINTED OR DISCONTENT WITH AND WHY?

_____
_____
_____
_____
_____

HOW CAN YOU RESOLVE, HEAL OR CHANGE WHAT YOU FEEL DISAPPOINTED OR DISCONTENT WITH? OR, HOW CAN YOU SUPPORT YOURSELF AT THIS TIME IF A RESOLUTION,CHANGE OR HEALING IS NOT POSSIBLE AT THIS TIME?

_____
_____
_____
_____
_____

WHAT BROUGHT YOU JOY, PEACE, CONTENTMENT AND/OR HAPPINESS?

WHAT DO YOU FEEL PROUD OF OR PROUD OF YOURSELF FOR?

_____
_____
_____

Mental Check In:

| HOW DO YOU FEEL MENTALLY RIGHT NOW? |

What is contributing to how you feel Mentally?

_____
_____

LIST ANY RECURRING THOUGHTS YOU RECALL HAVING.

_____

_____

_____

WHAT MIGHT THESE RECURRING THOUGHTS BE TELLING YOU? WHAT CAN YOU GLEAN FROM THEM?

_____

_____

_____

LIST ANY LIMITING BELIEFS OR LIMITING THOUGHTS YOU RECALL HAVING.

_____

_____

_____

HOW CAN YOU CHALLENGE OR REFRAME EACH OF THE ABOVE?

_____

_____

_____

Spiritual Check In:

HOW DO YOU FEEL SPIRITUALLY RIGHT NOW?

What is contributing to how you feel spiritually?

_____

_____

PROGRESSION THOUGH REFLECTION

WHAT DRAINED YOUR ENERGY ?	WHAT GAVE YOU ENERGY ?
_____	_____
_____	_____
_____	_____
_____	_____

Did you feel fully grounded and present?　　　　◯ Yes　　◯ No

If yes, what contributed to this feeling?

_____

If no, how can you foster more presence and ground yourself?

_____

Did you honor your boundaries?　　　　　　　　　◯ Yes　　◯ No

If no, how can you better honor your boundaries moving forward?

_____

Did you honor your values and priorities?　　　　◯ Yes　　◯ No

If yes, how? Was it in the way you expected and if not, how did it differ from your expectations?

_____

If no, what got in the way and how can you better honor your values and priorities moving forward?

_____

HOW DID YOU NUTURE YOURSELF?
(Food, rest, movement, connection, spiritual practice, grounding, creativity, play, fun, other.)

_____

IS THERE ANYTHING YOU NEED RIGHT NOW THAT YOU ARE NOT GIVING YOURSELF?

_____

_____

Check in with your goals & progress:
DID YOU TAKE ANY STEPS TOWARDS ANY OF YOUR GOALS OR DO ANYTHING SMALL THAT ALIGNS WITH THE BIGGER VISION YOU HAVE FOR YOURSELF ?　◯ Yes　◯ No

If yes, how? If no, what got in the way and what can you do differently tomorrow?

_____

_____

LIST ANY GOALS THAT NEED MORE ATTENTION:

_____

_____

LIST A SMALL STEP YOU CAN TAKE TOMORROW TOWARDS EACH TO GET THE BALL ROLLING.

_____

_____

LOOK BACK AT THE HABITS YOU ARE WORKING TO BUILD OR BREAK IN YOUR WEEKLY REFLECTION. HOW DID YOU DO? WHERE DID YOU SHOW DISCIPLINE AND WHERE DID YOU DEFAULT?

_____

_____

_____

IF YOU DEFAULTED BACK TO A HABIT YOU ARE TRYING TO BREAK, HOW CAN YOU REINFORCE YOUR WHY AND/OR MOVE FORWARD IN A MORE ALIGNED WAY? IS THERE A SMALLER STEP YOU CAN TAKE FIRST THAT WOULD MAKE THE TRANSITION EASIER OR FEEL LEST RESISTANT?

_____

_____

_____

DID YOU LEARN ANYTHING NEW ABOUT YOURSELF, YOUR GOALS, THE WAY YOU TRACK PROGRESS OR SOMETHING ELSE? IF SO, WRITE IT DOWN BELOW.

_____

_____

_____

USE THE SPACE BELOW FOR ANY ADDITIONAL NOTES:

TAKE A MOMENT TO AFFIRM THE FOLLOWING:
I am exactly where I need to be right now. I fully accept myself as I am, where I am. I am capable, focused, and moving forward with purpose. I celebrate today's wins and welcome tomorrow's opportunities. I release judgment. I am worthy of everything I desire.

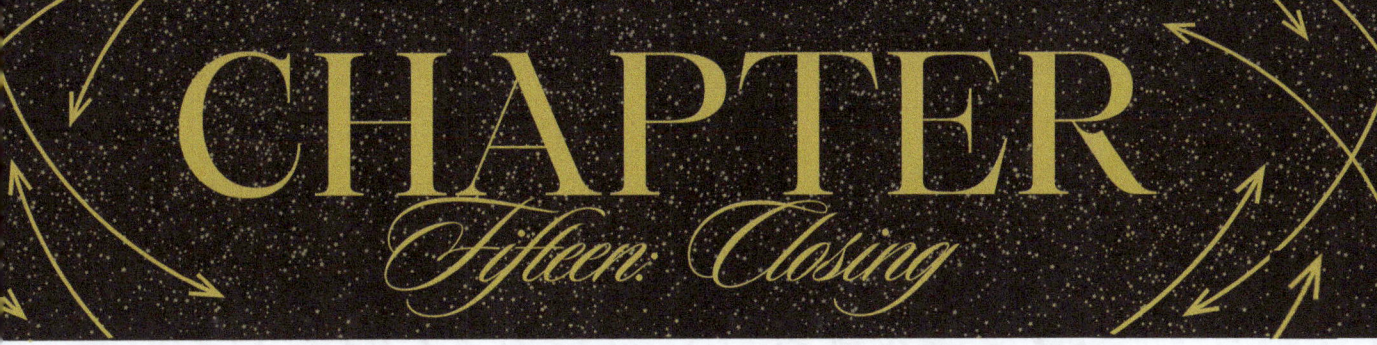

CHAPTER
Fifteen: Closing

CONGRATULATIONS ON COMPLETING YOUR 90-DAY JOURNEY!

Take a moment to honor how far you've come—the insights you've gained, the patterns you've noticed, and the progress you've made. Completing this journal is a testament not only to your commitment to your success but also to your commitment to yourself. And that is something truly worth celebrating!

As you move forward, carry the lessons, awareness, and practices you've cultivated here. Continue to show up for yourself with compassion, curiosity, and self-love.

What habits or practices had the biggest impact on you?

List 5 wins from the past 90 days—things you did, learned, or overcame.

_____

_____

_____

_____

_____

List any insights you gained over the last 90 Days:

Make your own list of affirmations to close your 90 day practice:

Thank-you!

To All My Valued Readers,

I want to take a moment to express my sincere gratitude to all of you. Each of your journeys is uniquely personal, and I feel deeply honored to have the opportunity to be a part of them. What you may not realize is that by joining this community, you're contributing to a larger purpose. Your decision to purchase this book and your support through reviews and word of mouth are invaluable in helping me make a greater positive impact. Your involvement extends beyond personal growth—it's part of a collective effort to effect positive change, getting this journal in the hands of more people who need it. Thank you for being a vital part of this shared mission and for your ongoing support. Publishing this journal has been a dream come true and you have been instrumental in the manifestation of that dream.

I wish you continued joy as you continue on your journey. And as always, may your life be full of light, full of love, gratitude and abundance.

Until We Meet Again,

Blake Hollaway

About
BLAKE C. HOLLAWAY

Blake C. Hollaway is a spiritual thought leader, transformation and manifestation coach, and the author of *The Break Up Journal: A Guide to Get Over Your Ex and Fall Back in Love with Yourself.* Inspired by her own journey of surviving abuse and self-recovery, Blake helps others embrace healing, intentional living, and personal empowerment. Her work blends spiritual practices with practical guidance, encouraging growth that is both grounded and transformative. Find Blake at www.blakechollaway.com or on social media @blakechollaway.

ACKNOWLEDGEMENTS

Thank you to my mom, without whom this book would not have been possible. Your unwavering support has been a constant source of encouragement throughout the years, especially during the process of writing and publishing this book. You taught me how to define life on my own terms and how to fight impossible battles. Your support in all these moments has provided me with the resilience and strength that ultimately paved the way for the creation of these pages, as well as many others, and will now light a path for so many others through the darkness.